The Braying Donkey:

Reflections on a Life

Timir Banerjee

BRANDYLANE PUBLISHERS, INC.

White Stone, Virginia

❋ Brandylane Publishers, Inc.
P.O. Box 261, White Stone, Virginia 22578
(804) 435-6900 or 1 800 553-6922; e-mail: brandy@crosslink.net

Library of Congress Cataloging-in-Publication Data

Banerjee, Timir, 1943-
    The braying donkey / Timir Banerjee.
        p.   cm.
    ISBN 1-883911-43-5
    1. Banerjee, Timir, 1943- 2. Neurosurgeons--United States--Biography.
3. Neurosurgeons--India--Biography. I. Title

RD592.9.B36 A3 2000
617.4'81'092--dc21
[B]   00-037907

This book is dedicated to "my girl"
who has encouraged me.

PREFACE

This is a story written with a pencil of love. I have taken liberty to exercise my fertile mind in expressing my love of the two countries (India, my country of birth, and America, my adopted country) that have given me a home and also have become a part of me. The Spirit blesses me, and I am waiting for more opportunities. As I write the story of my life, I find that my dream has truly come true. I am grateful to everyone who has shared love and joy with me. I am content, have no unfulfilled needs or wants, and want to honor my forefathers by following in their footsteps and renouncing all the greed attached to the gifts that I have received during my journey as I slowly meld into His ocean of love.

INTRODUCTION

This book is written with the belief that my failures have helped me grow. This is both truth and fiction, and it is up to the reader to make the distinction.

I understand that to some people life consists of "sound and fury, signifying nothing," as Shakespeare so eloquently wrote in *Macbeth*. However, I am convinced that there is indeed significance to my life although it seems I didn't make my mark. The sounds I made at life's disappointments and my moaning and groaning as life evolved have been similar to the braying of a donkey. Donkeys bray when they sense potential danger, but they also bray for joy, and the sounds are similar. My pain and suffering were real, but I have also felt joy beyond my comprehension, I believe, because God has a special purpose in my life and He has blessed me, a blessing I didn't fully deserve. I have overcome the pain and have come to understand the "blessing of pain," as Dr. Paul Brandt has explained. Now I am content knowing that Grace is free and I didn't have to earn it. My faith has led me as close to satchitanand (contentment and inner peace) as possible under any circumstances. I

have learned truly to enjoy life. As George Santayana writes in
his *A Minuet on Reaching the Age of Fifty,*

> If we confess our sins, they are forgiven
> We triumph, if we know we failed.
> Tears that in youth you shed,
> Congealed to pearls, now deck your silvery hair;
> Sighs breathed for loves long dead
> Frosted the glittering atoms of the air
> >   Into the veils you wear
> Round your soft bosom and most queenly head;
> >   The shimmer of your gown
> Catches all tints of autumn, and the dew
> Of gardens where the damask roses blew.

I am ready to celebrate life. Lakhyam!

We had been lovers for almost five years. "Do you know what ingredients I need to make hollandaise sauce?" he asked me. We were both grocery shopping. I told him. We exchanged names. He called me after a couple of weeks and invited me to dinner. I have a boyfriend, I told him. "Wednesday night is not a date night," he said softly in reply. I thought that to be true and enticing. We met in front of a grocery shop because I didn't want him to know where I lived yet. During dinner, after the small talk was over, he recited from Kahlil Gibran. We talked about *That Hideous Strength* by C. S. Lewis. We sipped sherry as we talked about Lord Feverstone and Curry in *Dinner with the Sub-Warden*. Somehow Nathaniel Hawthorne came up. I knew it was time to go home. My boyfriend was coming in around 11:30 P.M. from out of town. When I got home that night, I broke up with my boyfriend.

He had joined a practice about twenty-five years ago and had retired early to work in a different environment. "I have many things to do and I want to do them before I am old," he often said to me. We hiked. We traveled. I sometimes complained about the accommodations. He told me that it was better than sleeping with Queequeg at the Spouter Inn as Melville had described in *Moby Dick*. He massaged me with sensory therapy oil to sooth my discomfort. I sang Aretha Franklin's "You Make Me Feel Like a Natural Woman." I fell in love. We often read to each other, discussed the Bible, and prayed together for our children. "God developed a lot of understanding about his children only after His son Christ was born," he often said. "Read Jeremiah and you will see the wrath of an angry God, but then when we read John, we understand the loving parent," he said.

He was often gone, working in different countries. It was almost eight weeks after his death when I received the autopsy report. The doctor in Honduras wrote, "A severe wound to the neck" was the cause of his death. He died in a machete attack by the husband of a woman he was caring for outside San Pedro Sula. The husband allegedly didn't want his wife to live. She had been adulterous. The ER doctor remembers hearing "No operación mi esposa—morte!"

Ram was in the way of a drunken man's expression of violence. His body was cremated as instructed by the note in his billfold. His daughter picked up his ashes to be scattered in the river Mondakini (a river in northern India), as per the instructions in his will. I was the executor of his will. I rummaged through his belongings to make sure his possessions were properly distributed. In his desk drawer, I found a manuscript. I filled in parts from my memory to make his story complete. He was a friend. I loved his dreams and admired his goals. "Everybody for some reason helps me," he often said. I believed him. His patients loved him.

• • • • •

I was destined to be a physician. My father was one and so was my mother's father. I knew about stethoscope, otoscope, and blood pressure cuff as a youngster. I learned about tuberculosis and the importance of hydration in cases of diarrhea before I knew that the soccer ball leather becomes more pliable if greased with lard. I don't want you to think that my childhood was robbed or such, nor do I want you to presume that owing to all this learning at an early age I suffered from all kinds of neurotic symptoms as I got older. On the contrary, my childhood was like any other child, but with an added flavor of love from my grandfather. The intensity of our love for each other made the relationship so unique that everyone of my age was envious because such closeness was beyond their imagination.

Nobody knew my name, but everyone knew where I belonged. I was liked by most of the older fellows in my town, but many of the boys of my age hated me. And I knew that because they always kicked me on the shin while playing soccer and made it look like an accident. But I knew better. Older people didn't believe that what I felt was the truth because I was not a good soccer player anyway. I hated their preconceived judgmental attitudes. They always thought that I was expecting preferential treatment. Although secretly I always wanted that, I didn't want anyone to say it. It was a deception. I wanted it to happen. I had gotten used to it without recognizing it. Therefore, when it did not happen, I missed the advantage.

It took me many years to grow out of this attitude. Even after acknowledging this weakness, it took an active effort on my part to overcome this self-aggrandizing egocentricity. There was nothing special about me at all except that I was born into a family that was considered to be of the highest caste and financially successful.

It became more difficult to overcome the attitude of

conceit after I became a neurosurgeon. I became transformed from a class of privilege based on heritage to a class of accomplished persons with a large amount of vanity and narcissistic conceit. It was not until I found my God that I was able to change. My behavior pattern consisted of premature ejaculation of a vitriolic temperament that acted as a veil covering a psychological impotence. I was the captive of a demon that polluted my very being, but with effort I was able to demolish the destructive macabre despot from my soul. I became free to love and be loved. It was too late by then, and the lover of my youth decided to leave me in the harvest time of my life. She had found grounds that were more fertile and more easily tillable without the unnecessary smoking backfire of an old Caterpillar. My puritanical attitude was seeped with hypocrisy. Moreover, my disposition added crunchiness to the manipulating toast that I devoured daily. I was unable to forgive for the weaknesses of youth. I felt slighted. There was a sense of hidden vengeance that expressed itself much like Lord Byron's feeling of love: "From a welter of sound, it darted up like a bird/One authentic note of immortal longing." I was just out of control. This is what led to the greatest loss of my life. I failed to recognize the signs. I didn't pay heed to Alfred, Lord Tennyson when he said,

> It is the little rift within the lute,
> That by and by will make the music mute.

She was my girl for twenty-six years. She is the mother of my children. When we were younger we could not afford disposable diapers. She often sent me to the laundromat with a large number of soiled diapers for washing. I carried out the job most reluctantly. She worked on Dr. R. Zollinger's floor, and this usually meant she had to deal with residents who were chronically scared. All the residents usually have a special respect for their colleagues' wives and sometimes assume that they can be rescued under trying circumstances. She shared with me that one of the residents (now a professor of surgery) had asked her to administer a Phenergan suppository for nausea to a patient. Subsequently, during rounds, Dr. Zollinger expressed his dislike for Phenergan. The resident doctor, suspecting a possible rebuke for his action from Dr. Zollinger, asked her to extricate the suppository out of the patient. I remember my colleague telling me that my wife failed to perform this miracle on his behalf.

We worked together in almost everything in life. At least I tried to participate whenever I could with my limited time. She allowed me special favors. I recall watching on TV the astronauts landing on the moon exactly at the time of our climactic howl. She knew I liked cherry delite, a dessert with cherries and graham crackers, and used to make the dessert for me and hide it under the bed. She had found out that otherwise the babysitter would eat up the whole dessert before I came home from the hospital.

She loved animals, and, therefore, we almost had a little zoo in our yard. We laid sod together. She even weeded the garden and hauled brush. She confided in me that her father made her haul brush, and she hated it. I tried to do that chore subsequently. She mowed the yard. She painted the rooms. She even ironed my shirts and pillowcases. We pasted wallpaper together. One time a neighbor said, "You guys will be always together. Anybody that don't kill each other while placing wallpaper on the ceiling are sealed for life." She cooked. She entertained. She was often alone when I would have to leave in the middle of a party to see patients in the emergency room.

She always understood. She didn't like to play bridge, but she played because I liked it. She knew how to fix faucets. She designed our home. She even knew how to make a veloute (the round structure in the beginning of stairway railings. She knew how to make the velouté sauce as well.)

We played tennis together. She didn't like me telling her that there was a hole in her racquet when she missed the ball. She was my secretary and my nurse. I told her that I loved her as my secretary because I could come in the back room and make out for awhile. She was a good sport. She was my entertainment. She was my soulmate. She was my love. She was my life. At times, I feel sad that I didn't do more things that she liked.

However, I overcame the grief that followed as I learned progressively to be free and caring. Now I am able to share my joy with others. I have learned not to expect someone else to meet my criterion to gain acceptance in his or her arena of life. I will never be a Daniel, but I understand now that the lions are a part of life. I have realized that only the gifted can tame them, but I have learned to love them despite their roar, which is frightening at times. I prayed silently, and God has filled my life with *anand* (Sanskrit word for the ultimate joyful state) in my heart. I didn't exactly know then what it was that I needed, but I have realized that all my needs and wants have been met.

I wanted a life like a Monet painting. I wanted to explore the uneven and complex paint surfaces and admire the play of light across the water surface. I dreamed that the lilies moistened by the fresh dew of the morning in their colorful lingerie while floating and flirting with the misty sunlight would wink at me. I dreamed of a life where I would wake up every morning with my lover in my arms. I wished to look at her face with a new energy and a renewed vigor to enjoy the glory again. I wanted to accomplish my goals before it was too late. I remember reading Keats.

> The weariness, the fever, and the fret
> Here, where men sit and hear each other groan;
> Where palsy shakes a few, sad, last gray hairs,
> Where youth grows pale, and specter-thin, and dies;
> Where but to think is to be full of sorrow
> And leaden-eyed despairs,
> Where beauty cannot keep her lustrous eyes,
> Or new Love pine at them beyond tomorrow.

I wanted to remain active as long as I could while, as William Wordsworth wrote, I still felt as though "my heart leaps up when I behold a rainbow in the sky/A rainbow so was it when my life began; so is it now I am a man."

After residency, I went to India to find a suitable opportunity. The system of medical profession seemed to be seeping with bureaucratic procedures. The attitude of the officials didn't permit free communication. I was unable to determine my usefulness in my country of birth. My wife and I were frustrated by the general reception and basically decided against going to India to work on a full-time basis. I still remembered the *gundas* (hired bouncers to beat up others) who attacked me when I was the president of the students' union. I spoke with directness, honesty, and candor, and that did not help me gain support. I lacked the polish of diplomacy. I hadn't quite learned the value and effectiveness of the diplomatic smile. I remembered the time when I was running for reelection in the students' union and how heated our campaign had become. One evening, some unknown assailants apprehended us right outside the medical school and left me lying unconscious on the street.

However, I don't dwell on such topics.

I was ready to settle down in life with the intent to be useful to myself as well as to others. I had an attitude and a behavior pattern that fostered friendship, and a sense of discipline that could drive me.

I knew that happiness is not for tomorrow but to be had today. As I progressively felt content with myself, I knew that I wanted to work as a volunteer. I wanted to be involved in such an endeavor before all my hair was gray and my vision was distorted from cataracts. I understood at an early age the difference between happiness and success. But I was not successful in maintaining a balance in my life. In the middle of the journey, I realized I had chased these two elusive phenomena riding the chariot of work.

I never contemplated nor did I formulate any plan to be successful. I just worked, remaining oblivious of most other activities surrounding my life. However, I did realize that happiness was not to be found in possession but in renunciation, whereas success meant power and wealth. I must admit that during my youthful years it was difficult for me to understand exactly what that meant. I also did not comprehend the feeling of "not possessing," because all the while I was possessing I was not conscious of it. It is not something that I thought of or dwelled upon much. I always thought success came naturally with hard work. I always remembered my father saying, "Don't chase money; it is elusive. But just work hard and it will chase you." My father was very perceptive.

It was made clear to me as a child that I had to persevere, and that a laissez-faire attitude is not to be had in life.

I learned to care about everything, and the words "whatever" and "I don't care" hadn't made their way to India yet. My father and I often discussed the medieval country of

Cockayne and its relationship with heaven. But we never reached an agreement as to the way of reaching there. I learned about this place that is full of rivers of wine, houses built of cake and sugar, streets paved with pastry and where everything is free. Roasted geese wander about the streets inviting people to eat them and buttered birds fall from the sky like manna.

• • • • •

The concept of finding myself by going off-piste was not very popular during my childhood. It was generally felt that we should not get distracted during the years of study. However, I took a walk in the mountains by myself when I was about eighteen years old. During this walk, I discovered my desires and my needs, which have not changed much since then. I prayed loudly and yelled to God, hoping He would listen. There was no one else visible on my path at that time. I sat and contemplated and imagined myself surrounded with people whom I loved and who loved me. I felt something unique was happening. It was an aura of an impending escalation to heights I had never experienced before. This motorized ladder had no guardrails. As I sailed over valleys and rivers, the only sound I heard was the whispering of the wind as it captured the colorful sail while my mast remained steady and unshaken. I imagined a lover, a *yakshi* (women with large bosoms on the walls of the Khajuraho temple) who would entice me, engulf me, smother and tease me. Our playful chase would end on a bed of wildflowers, lying in a sweaty, rapturous embrace. A soft, gentle breeze would cool our skin while the songs of the birds lulled us to somnolence.

We would hear the flowers on the long stems not flattened by our enthusiastic gymnastics giggle and gossip about our jubilant loss of innocence. A few butterflies would fly by, shyly waving their wings. This was an expression of their approval. I was happy to have these pretty witnesses to our celebration of the beauty of love in this Garden of Eden.

I was tired after a long walk to reach here. As I lay down, I saw the giant rocks standing up with their mighty sinews protruding out, protecting the genteel meadow of wild flowers of Nandankanan (valley of flowers). A song much like music from *Camelot,* "how to handle a woman, simply love her," was playing in my ear. I had just walked out of the opera participating in exquisite gyrations while Ravi Shankar played "Raga Bhimpalasi" with accompaniment from the great Alla Rakka. Now, I heard only the soft sounds of a tender embrace as my yakshi lay next to me.

I saw this River Mondakini flowing and splashing and just running down to meet Alaknanda. In its youthful vigor and excitement, it tripped and glided but never complained. Instead, it bathed the surroundings with sprays of refreshing laughter. The thrilled trees expressed gaiety with music of the leaves while swaying in this joyful discotheque. Its consort, the wind, attracted by its energy, brought a veil of cloud to keep the sun away from its youthful countenance. The trees joined in the effort by making shadows on her body to protect it from the rays of the blistering sun of the higher elevations. It mesmerized the mountains as they stood still to admire this new flow of vibrant life captivating and sprinkling the virgin grounds with its sparkling breath. Having total control of the wind and the clouds, the sun played hide and seek on the pristine water. I heard the bass bassoon of Louis Armstrong simmering through the environment as the water rushed through the high hills to fall into cascading waterfalls.

In my pensive mood, like Wordsworth, I truly enjoyed

"the inward eye, which is the bliss of solitude" as "my heart danced with the daffodils" (William Wordsworth, "The Daffodils"). It is at this moment of exhilaration that I conceived my daughter and carried her until I was able to implant her in the womb of my yakshi, her mother-to-be, and named her Mondakini.

Later on, she needed a name her neighbors could pronounce more easily and also that would be more suited to the place where she grew up. She liked her grandmother's name, Marie, and thus my beautiful daughter of river and mountain, M&M, was delivered to this world.

• • • • •

I was not good in any sports. Whenever I played, no one ever passed the ball to me, although I played right out or center. I could dribble a little bit, but I was always afraid to hit the ball with my head like the other boys. I just could not kick it quickly enough, I guess. It seemed that every time I had the ball, one of the players from the opposite team took it away somehow. I had the boots and the socks and the colorful shorts to make me look interesting, but I just didn't have the kick to go with it. I tried to play volleyball, but I was afraid to hurt my hands. Somehow, I managed to play field hockey and a little bit of cricket. However, I never made the high school team or the varsity team, as it is called these days. Later, I learned that golf is the only game where I could have acquaintance with the ball the longest! I was able to overcome my sense of isolation from the ball and the feeling that I was being picked on by my classmates.

I decided that I was more of a card player on a green table than a ball player on the green grass. My *Da* (grandfather) always told me that a real man always knows his limitations.

• • • • •

I am often asked, "Where are you from?" I don't really know what they mean, and after a lot of thinking I realized that what they want to know is where I grew up. This is a difficult question to answer correctly because I have not grown up yet. I know that I have a lot of growing to do still in many aspects, although not necessarily physically. I thought when some people asked me that question they were trying to make me feel different, because the question contains an assumption that "you are not from here" or "we know everybody from here and they don't look like you or talk like you." Although some of the folks had that nefarious intention, most others asked that question just to start a conversation, or they did not know or understand what it implied. I realized it soon enough. I ran with it and overcame the chip on my shoulder. Some people actually wanted to know for sure so that they could say that they had been to India, and then possibly we would have a common ground for light conversation. Soon I started asking that question to others, and found that many people got offended, which confirmed my previous concept that those who asked me the question usually had a negative attitude toward me because I didn't look like them. I began to wonder why none of my friends ever asked me such a question before telling me first where they grew up.

I remember the time when I would have breakfast in the hospital cafeteria. This was a busy place in the morning because the doctors were allowed to have free breakfast. Many of the staff doctors came there as well. I was accosted by many who would ask me bizarre questions. I answered them rather politely at first. However, later I thought I should play a little game with them. I was not about to allow myself to be treated as someone asking for a handout. Mind you, these people were from a part of America that has had biases for generations against anyone from any place besides their own community. My reading indicated that this provincial bigotry extended to such a point that they often bore grudges against anyone who thought differently or disagreed with them. They didn't want me to blend in.

I felt that these people would like me to be excluded rather than have me included in their club. Many of the people I met still maintained an antebellum attitude in their interactions toward anyone new in the area. I was fully aware that I needed to flatter many of them so that they would write decent recommendation letters for me, which would be essential for my success in America. I also knew that people with biases are easily flattered by platitudes.

I had come to America alone and did not know anyone. I obviously had a lot to learn about myself as well as the behavior of the new people around me. I remember one time one of the staff had asked me if I saw snakes and tigers everyday next to my house. I told him that the tigers controlled the traffic when the snakes crossed the streets. For some reason he did not ask me any questions after that.

I met a medical resident many years later in Zimbabwe while working as a lecturer. He shared with me that during a rotation in Manchester, England, someone had asked him if people in Africa wore clothes. He said that he was very offended. I suggested that it is important for him to take advantage of the capitalist society—that fostering and promoting such benign ignorance would bring more tourists to Africa; moreover, that anger was a luxury only a child could afford. We both laughed. We talked about Eleanor Roosevelt and the fact that she said,

"No one can insult you if you don't want to be insulted." I shared with him a little bit of Henry James, who had said, "American men had the elements of modern man with the culture left out," fully realizing that this appeared as an expression of bitterness. However, it seemed like an opportunity to vent my feelings, particularly as I had experienced some condescension as well.

I had traveled much by then. I was under the impression that traveling is supposed to broaden our horizons and improve the mind. However, I found that many men of my adopted country believed, "We have not as much refinement, but more of everything that is good." I grew up with the concept that arrogance was a sign of ignorance, and I was under the impression that humility was a sign of good breeding. I made every effort so that I would not have an irreverent impression of my newly adopted country.

I also made a sincere effort not to say anything disparaging to some of the people who often provoked me in a manner that challenged my tolerance. I was not in a position to make any judgment about discrimination. The discriminator often does not realize and lacks the sensitivity necessary to lift up the one being discriminated. I was at the other end now in a new country, and I wanted to be American about it. Here we are not supposed to have a class distinction, although some of us might have believed that we were either born into a superior class or into a superior color or lack of it. I took it as a challenging sport and tried to find a solution for it. I changed my perception and made it a point not to be discriminated against by acknowledging that the improper behavior directed toward me was a weakness of character. I asked God to forgive them for their shortcomings. I am ashamed to admit that most of the time this very act gave me a sense of superiority, and I felt more in control. I never felt discriminated against subsequently, although some people treated me unkindly at times.

I wanted to make everyone an emulsion of my milk. I did not approve of those who placed vinegar in the relationships and curdled the milk, separating the whey from the casein. I realized that learning to negotiate in a diplomatic manner and an attitude of acceptance was all that was necessary to adapt to this new environment. I felt that it was a fair game to take advantage of the weaknesses of those who refused to give me "a seat in the home that is not my own" (Rabindranath Tagore, "Gitanjali.")

I started making fun of people for entertainment. I recall that a gentleman who had gotten to know me a bit from our previous encounter winked at me once as a gesture of acknowledgment when he saw me in a hallway. I smiled back and asked him if there was something wrong with his eyes because I had noticed a spasm. In our subsequent meetings in the hall, I believe our greetings had been in an audible spoken language. It seemed that I sometimes lashed out and victimized innocent people much the same way others were treating me at times. I began making progress, and my color was not a barrier to me or to anyone else.

I was in a country where color, caste, and class were three five-letter words that were not supposed to exist. I was not in England, where either you had to be born into a class or had to have a certificate to be a gentleman. I was not in India, where you had to be born into a superior caste to qualify to be a high-class person. I was in America. It is only here that I could excel by my own actions. It is only here that individuality is respected. I had given up certain advantages of my life that would be considered quite valuable to some others. I wanted an identity of my own. I wanted to start a new generation. I had embarked on an adventure. I had already read *Pygmalion*. The movie *Trading Places* hadn't been made yet. I thought that having a little color could not have been that big a deal as I had watched many people lay naked on the beach to get roasted just to get a little color. Then I realized that this effort is possibly similar to the time I got a tattoo on my arm. I was once excited about having a "little Suzie" tattooed on my upper arm. I thought it would be a conversation piece when I would sit in the doctor's lounge wearing my scrubs. I didn't want it for all my life. Therefore, I made sure it was a special stamped tattoo that would go away after a few showers.

There have been times when the attitude of vindictiveness of the Count of Monte Cristo welled up within me. However, God helped me to control the negative spirit and transformed the energy in a positive way for my future benefit. I know that with privilege comes an implicit responsibility to be cordial, hospitable, and helpful. I wanted to be a true American, such that I would consider it a privilege to be able to help others. I thought that this act should not be considered as a duty and, therefore, did not expect a thank-you.

• • • • •

It is not uncommon to fall into a ditch while driving on the snowy roads of Wisconsin. As a matter of fact, anybody who hasn't driven in the ditch at least once probably hasn't lived there long enough or is too shy to admit it. Strangers stop and give a push, and they don't wait to be thanked. They just go on their merry way of sliding but taking their foot off the brakes at times to avoid the same situation happening to them.

In America, we do not say to anything, "It cannot be done." Here people say, "I don't know how, but I will find out," and then there is a sincere effort to figure it out. Here people are free of rank except in the armed forces. I was in San Diego Naval Hospital during one of my ACDUTRA duties when my captain reminded me to be careful in the operating room as to how I expressed myself because the nurse scrubbing with me could be my superior officer. In the event that I was less than polite or condescending during an operation, the slighted person could very well have ruined my evenings and the rest of my stay during this term of active duty. Of course, this is all part of the game.

No one I know bears any grudge about a slip in the operating room. I must admit it was kind of fun getting saluted when I was a commander.

• • • • •

I had an opportunity to meet several interesting persons while I was in the navy, but I had met my friend Larry before joining the navy. He is a two-star admiral and a truly benevolent man.

I love my admiral friend, Mr. L. Franklin. He has served in Vietnam and has commissioned several submarines. He has never forgotten his roots, and, despite all the honors that have been bestowed upon him, he likes to lift the other person. We have had many a martini together and have shared exaggerated stories and laughter until late in the evenings. He has taught me humility, and he does not know it, but I have prayed for him. I love him like my own brother. I am glad he is my friend, particularly because he is a fierce attorney who makes a living suing doctors.

It has been a few years since I received a copy of a letter from an insurance company that one of the attorneys had written to them. One particular attorney had expressed his displeasure about me in writing after I had examined a client of his in a workmen's compensation case. This gentleman client had claimed a back condition subsequent to an injury while working in a church building. I was unable to detect any objective findings and suggested that he could possibly return to work. I had also learned that despite his painful calamity, he was able to make frequent social visits to the minister's daughter. I knew that we live in a country where no one is above the law, and we can even impeach a president. My attorney friend told me that we could not sue the ill-tempered attorney for calling me an idiot. However, we could sue him if I felt insulted after having been addressed as a charlatan. I was thrilled, and we pursued the case. I told this name-calling attorney that I had developed a problem with confidence ever since he called me a name, and that it would improve only with a financial settlement. He knew that I could play the game well.

I did not need any money, but we had him make a significant donation dictated by the court directly to the university to have a lecture on ethics in law. I accepted a written apology as well for the fun of it.

I believe that sometimes people get carried away with their newly discovered power. I lived on a property with no neighbors for more than ten years in the early seventies. I had a big St. Bernard, Bennie, who liked to roam the neighborhood, which was about ten acres away. I knew there was a leash law in effect somewhere. Nevertheless, I felt it was inappropriate to keep my dog confined in this property when there were ten acres of unused land for the canine pleasure of chasing rabbits. As a matter of fact, Bennie was so harmless that once she had allowed the entry of a whole baby rabbit, face first, into her mouth, but did not swallow it. I could tell that she was proud of this accomplishment and wanted a "that-a-gal," I suppose. Bennie always was very strong in her appearance, yet most gentle. The predicament of the rabbit reminded me of a story that I had heard as a child. The story of the rabbit has a great similarity to my life. It will become apparent as the story unfolds that I, too, felt cramped in my quarters in the beginning, and then, slowly, became liberated in my new habitat as I began to feel familiar with my surroundings.

She just let the rabbit loose after she came in the house, and the little bunny just backed out. I do not know what the rabbit felt or thought of while traveling in the warmth of the inside of the mouth of a giant enemy. I am sure that it looked at the inside of the throat at the two openings and couldn't decide which was the road less traveled by while she breathed the hot air generated by the dog's excitement at this lively catch. I believe Jonah might have felt similarly while traveling inside the whale. I wished I could have eavesdropped under the flowering cherry bush to hear her talk to her mom about the exciting day she had while her stepsiblings would be saying, "Tell me another one," not even taking their eyes off "The X-Files."

But Xanadu held Annabel close to her chest and let her stop panting. She had dozed off a little, being tired at the end of the day. She thought of her friend Shabnam (a Persian name meaning morning dew).

At first, Shabnam was skeptical about their relationship, particularly for having different appearances. But soon they began to develop their friendship owing to the fact that they were both eating from the same garden every day. They began to share each other's experiences in this new land. Shabnam was a beautiful snail and had a lot of confidence. One sunny day, when they were merely exercising their freedom of choice by eating snapdragons and kale, Shabnam pointed out the camouflaged cans of Budweiser in the garden. She told Xanadu never to go near them. She continued that the owner of the garden did not approve of her cousins, the slugs. Slugs by nature love sliding, but they were drowned while playing on this enticing sliding board of slippery cans filled with an aromatic fluid.

Now, being an American she began to feel this to be an attractive nuisance. She felt that there should be something done about it. Xanadu loved the American spirit in her friend, particularly when she heard how in America everyone could realize his or her dream by just working for it. Shabnam shared this secret desire to go to a car dealer with Xanadu. She also wanted to get a personalized license plate saying "S" on it. Then, she thought, it would be fun if she could drive out of the lot before Xanadu and go really fast on the expressway where there would be no speed limit. She wanted for once everybody to say, "Look at that 'S' car go."

Xanadu remembered that Annabel was the first born. She had plucked the hair from her chest and had prepared this soft bed by making layers of cotton on a pile of leaves of gardenia and bay magnolia. She thought that this would deliver a fresh aroma in her place of birthing, inside the deep hole underneath the pear tree. She knew of the black snake that lived nearby. She was never sure exactly where it lived because it could go into much smaller holes. She was envious of Shabnam because there are no snail-eating snakes in America. But Xanadu was pleased that despite being from a different culture and being new in the neighborhood, Joyce and Jennifer's family was friendly and helped her through the difficult times. Mostly, she knew from her past experience that

So twice five miles of fertile ground
With walls and towers were girdled round:
And there were gardens bright with sinuous rills,
Where blossomed many an incense bearing tree
    (Samuel Taylor Coleridge, "Kubla Khan")

She had placed sticks near the openings so that slightest motions suggesting danger would wake her up. She had six little hairless beautiful babies, but the slimy snake took them all except Annabel. When Annabel heard her mother's heartbeat, she calmed down and described her experience.

She was inside a partially illuminated cave, which had a soft slobbery floor, and the roof had ridges that squeezed on her back and the walls were made of large dentition that locked in like the gates in the castle of Theseus. The castle seemed extraordinarily guarded, much like at the time of the new moon in May when Hippolyta, queen of the Amazons, was expected to be married. Her nose touched a soft tickler, which looked like a hathi gray that almost made her sneeze.

She held out as long as she could, and she was afraid to breathe. She saw in front of her, far down below, a boiling cauldron of gastric juice, and although she did not know much about haute cuisine or hasenpfeffer, this area just did not look safe. When she looked into the other opening, it was like an accordion moving air through a hole filled with white slime. This reminded her of the time when her curiosity took her to the barn, and she had slipped on a pile left over after the lamb was born. The place was so confining that she could not even move her tail, and that made her feel rather uncomfortable because that's one particular act that made her feel powerful. She felt consoled when her mother told her about a love that happened many years ago near the ocean. She fell asleep while listening to

> For the moon never beams without bringing me dreams
> Of the beautiful Annabel Lee . . .
>   (Edgar Allen Poe, "Annabel Lee")

Bennie hated the thunder, and whenever it rained, which was not uncommon in June, this 160-pound cuddly dog would run into the nearest kitchen, and often it wasn't ours.

Everybody loved Bennie, except the new lawyer who sent out a notice to implement the leash law. Bennie, of course, could not read the leaflets attached to the mailbox. Moreover, she was very polite and she never read anyone else's mail.

So she did not follow any rules and continued to enjoy her freedom. As luck would happen to anyone whose heart is pure, I saw a little pooch in our yard one day when I came home from work. I told my son to tie him up to the fence next to the doghouse and give him some water and food. I introduced a law, to be effective immediately, that no one could have the dog unless "the daddy of the house spoke to my dad."

My son stuck a sign saying as such on the fence so that we would not have to hire a policeman from the city for the implementation of this newly proclaimed law. A few days later, when my wife and I were working outside laying down some sod next to our swimming pool, a man drove up in a Land Rover and introduced himself as the owner of the dog. He expressed a desire to reimburse us for any damages his dog might have caused. I knew that he was the attorney who had passed out the restricting leaflet that had aroused my negative energy. I remembered that my professor had told me that in life it always hurts more "when one gets hit with a Rolls Royce than by a

Volkswagen." I showed him the canine footprints on the newly laid sod. I informed him that he could not afford to pay for all the damages because ever since the dog came to our yard it had laid indelible marks on my heart in addition to the ones on the grass. I also felt that it would require prolonged psychotherapy to erase these dog marks. We both laughed, and he removed the leaflets that Bennie could not read. We shared a box of bourbon bonbons to celebrate the opportunity of making acquaintance. Now, Bennie found a new friend, and we became better Americans in our brotherhood.

• • • • •

I found that in my life friendships have been abounding, and I have benefited immensely from the opportunities given me. I have discovered that honorable people respect equality, and many persons have helped me find a solution to a problem together. This is the spirit of an American. When I lived in Wisconsin, I had an old stethoscope that needed replacement. I had it for seventeen years and I loved it. When I learned that the local people did not understand my attachment for it and just wanted to sell me a new one, I wrote to the president of the 3M company. He sent me a replacement part with his compliments in less than a week.

American business listens to its consumers. I was using a dye for myelograms (a test to see the spinal column) that came in 50cc bottles. But we used only 20cc of the medicine and the rest was being thrown away. I wrote to the president of the company saying that we should not be wasteful. The next batch was made in new 25cc bottles for general distribution. I love this America where we are all part of it. During my short stay in India, I knew that this type of assistance and communication between physicians and industry would have been impossible. It is my guess that the secretary would never have allowed me to speak to her busy boss.

I had already read much of Whitman, Twain, and Steinbeck. I have always believed that reading is the heart and soul of culture in its highest form, but to my surprise some of the persons who were feeling superior to me had not even read all their works. There were even some who had not seen any of Jackson Pollock's paintings. I have been invigorated by his paintings. He has been one of my favorites with his innovative display of colors expressing a pervasive energy and an acquisition and announcement of the freedom of spirit.

I knew that everyone in this country was from somewhere else, and by making the best use of their talents and thus by promoting and enhancing America, they became Americans. I still remember President Kennedy's speech, " . . . ask not what your country can do for you—ask what you can do for your country." I had read most of the Constitution, and about the importance of its concept of equality of all men.

Here in America we are all Americans, even if we are naturalized citizens and didn't make the choice of being born here. This is not a forged painting or counterfeit money status. We are all equal under the law where the government is truly "of the people, by the people, for the people." I always felt very confident knowing this and understanding the important role it played to the writers of the Constitution when this great nation was being built.

The pride one feels in being an American and the honor that America bestows on its citizens distinguishes America from most other countries. It is the sense of belonging that all of us feel that has made America a truly diverse nation where people from different countries and cultures have come to be known as

Americans. It is almost like a religion where one can be proselytized into being an American. But there are no missionaries to attract anyone—only the beckoning call of true democracy.

I have had many opportunities as a neurosurgeon to travel and see the world. I had known from the anonymous writer of "The Penny and the Gingerbread," published in *Harper's* in 1928, that "any simpleton can save up his dollars, but the wisest of men cannot save up opportunities—they must be used as they come." I read voraciously while traveling as an adult. I believe this was a result of the encouragement to read as a youngster. I caught up on reading my medical journals while traveling. I published a monthly pamphlet, *Neuro News,* summarizing multiple journals and mailed copies to my colleagues who referred patients to me.

I have fished in the crystal clear, ice cold waters of Great Bear Lake, where the shores become invisible very shortly after taking off on a boat. The only way to be found, if lost, is by making a smoke signal from the distant shore and hoping that some one will see it. Here the famished mosquitoes are in a constant feeding frenzy, and it is wise to tuck the pants inside the socks and wear a mosquito net on the head while eating unless one desires some "wings" with eggs in the morning. The trout are big, and they like to participate in a good tug-of-war at the end of the line. They certainly gave me a challenge, particularly because I didn't want to hurt their mouths and fished with a hook without a burr.

I have put up a pup tent in the tundra at the Arctic National Wildlife Refuge to see the caribou immersed up to its rack in the still waters of the braided Hula Hula River to avoid the penetrating proboscis of the swarming mosquito.

The musk oxen gallop and the grizzly roam in the

wilderness. They also enjoy the freedom in the "land of the free and the brave" that we all so proudly share. The energetic arctic tern and the shy fox make themselves visible in this flat Serengeti of the north, as do the other birds that live on this land with no trees. The sun keeps its lights on all day without a flicker. The wind and the rain chase each other, taking only occasional breaks for a breath, and the darkness of night is kept far away for six months of the year.

I have noticed farmers' wives sorting apples while the men are whittling and smoking corncob pipes in the backdoors of Carolina and Kentucky. They give each other orders only to make a living, and then the women tell tales and men say sweet nothings as they pass on to a state of deep somnolence right in the middle of a conversation. I don't believe the farmers ever need a sleeping pill. I am convinced that the hard work, freedom of choice, an honorable heart, and the family unity keep them from the insomnia that afflicts many of us.

I have played baseball from the back of mules during cold but precious sunny days in Wisconsin. I have raced on the back of a camel in the deserts of western India, although not as fast as depicted in *Lawrence of Arabia*. I have been titillated by the winking of the umbilicus of Arab beauty in the mystic restaurants of Casablanca during a heart-racing, erotic performance of belly dancing.

I have seen the lions make love and cheetahs chase their prey in the prairies of Serengeti. I have taken pictures of a leopard, sitting on top of a tree at Masai Mara, that didn't want to share its kill.

I have heard the tittering of hyenas as they were eating up a lion's meal. I have invited my partner to make love in the coupe of a 747. I have seen beauty in the back seat of a car, and I have dreamed of ménage à trois in my escapades.

I have seen the glow worms of Titiranga and the Blue Grotto of Capri.

I have driven through Bad Oldesloe and walked on the promenade of Travernude, along the windy harbor of the Baltic Sea on a cold February day. The sun was peeping through the comb of clouds. The individual spray of rays like pointed trabeculations poked the sun-deprived local dwellers into excitement as they walked along the windswept beach. Many celebrated the occasion by flying giant kites, to their ecstasy. These artificial birds sang and gyrated in the wind of the sea while men held down the strings with both hands. These men faced the wind. They held on to the strings with all their might. These colorful birds challenged the men by swaying with the music of Chubby Checker's twist while the crew dug their heels in the sand, holding on to their end in the tug-of-war.

The frustrated retriever dispersed its energy by barking incessantly at the gulls. The white birds, on the other hand, splashed and swung their wings, expressing their dissatisfaction. They did not approve of this intrusion during the time of quiet fishing in the afternoon.

I have been on a skidoo at Bayfield on Lake Superior. I have rolled naked in the snow for a thrill after running out of a sauna. However, I was dismayed to find myself in a state of complete refrigeration with all my appurtenances shriveled like a prune at a time when I thought excitement would prevail. My lover honored this act of lunacy with a gift of afternoon delight. Unfortunately, the chill of the cold weather left me limp and deprived me of a well-deserved bonus.

I have had my palm read by a Ph.D. in Jackson Square, and my tarot cards drawn by a bird in Nepal. I have tasted the bark of the cannabis from the *cheelum* (an hourglass-shaped clay utensil) of a *sadhu* (guru dressed in saffron colored outfit) at the HemKund. I even had the courage to sit in front of a witch doctor in Zimbabwe to learn about his methods.

I have seen a brain operation performed under acupuncture. I have been surprised to see the doctor clean up the room with a mop to get it ready for the next procedure! I have seen some of the destructive effects of the Cultural Revolution in China. I have seen the power of oppression on the faces of the people in China, Tibet, and Russia.

I have been in the tombs of Queen Nefreteri and King Tutankhamen and wondered about the power of blood holding the mortar to the bricks. I found it interesting that the local Egyptologists did not acknowledge the enslavement of the Jews. I think I came back and saw *Ben Hur* and the *Ten Commandments* again. I often wondered if my fascination was really for Moses or for Charleston Heston's rendition of Cecil B. DeMille's imagination. Regardless, I was fascinated, and I believe I saw the chariot race more than five times although I knew the result!

I have had the good fortune of listening to Beverly Sills and Pavarotti. I have seen William Tell at La Scala and beguiling, bouncing Baryshnikov at the Bolshoi Ballet. The classical dance of Uday Shanker, soul searching Sarod of Ustad Ali Akbar, and dinner at the White House at one of the Republican dinners with President Reagan have been part of all I tasted. I have wiped my tears while listening to Ravi Shankar play Bhairab Raga (Indian classical music). I have sat through the night with eyes closed under a tent to hear Ustad Alla Rakka play the Tabla, inviting the awakening sun through the silence of the night.

I have cherished my days of walking around the Trevi fountain and praying at St. Peter's Basilica. I have stood in St. Peter's Square on the first of January when the Pope blessed me. This memorable rinsing overjoyed me.

I have learned to enjoy the spirit of all-American "busy leisure," as Pitkin described it. I have worked hard during the leisure time to enjoy short periods of restful energy. I have learned to taste the meal consisting of work and play served on the same platter. I have been able to distinguish one from the other while enjoying both of them equally.

I have spent days admiring the works of art displayed in the Louvre, the Hermitage, and the Prado museums. I believe I have dreamed of becoming a connoisseur of art, but I am content with the fact that my ardent desire to understand art has at least led me to appreciate beauty.

I have watched the women on the beaches of Dubrovnik, Cancún, and Rio de Janeiro, and gambled at Monte Carlo and Baden-Baden. I have sipped on 1961 Chateau Lafite Rothschild and I have watched the cabaret at Moulin Rouge. I have run up the Eiffel Tower and dreamt of hang gliding off Grandfather Mountain of North Carolina.

I have driven to the Hanna, swam in the seven seas, and bicycled in the Catalina islands.

I have seen Michael Jordan play and Jackie Joyner-Kersee run, and I have heard Reba McIntyre sing "The Man Next to Me." I have seen the Blue Angels and *The Sound of Music,* and once I even took a nap among the edelweiss.

I have skied on the mountains of Colorado and at St. Moritz. I have snorkeled and sailed in the waters of the Pennycamp National Park, Caribbean, and La Digue, and I have played hide-and-seek in the baths of Virgin Gorda.

I have been early enough to see the sun rise over Cadillac Mountain and I have been on horseback to see the China Wall in the Bob Marshall wilderness.

I have driven along the avenues bordered with gulmohar,

jacaranda, and coral trees punctuated by trees bearing mangoes and guavas in the Seychelles. I have sat in the pastures of corn and watched the silky brown tufts of hair swing in the rain. I have watched the drangoes with wet feathers mark the wayside while the melodies of bulbul and mynah birds permeated the air.

I have taken fencing lessons. I have seen every Errol Flynn and Douglas Fairbanks Jr. movie. I have taken dancing lessons. I have dreamed of waltzing in King Ludwig's palace in Munich when the king would be riding his carriage in the courtyard.

I have seen the salmon jump and the whales spout. I have cooked marshmallows on a campfire and watched ducks fly with moon on their wings. I have canoed in Wonder Lake with my son, and we have quietly shared the colorful sunrise on Mt. McKinley with an apprehensive ptarmigan family.

I have tried to count the fish in the waters of Mahé during a chaotic excitement of feeding. I even met a man who has a job counting the fish in the rivers of Montana. He dampened my spirits in qualifying his credentials by informing me that he had connections and this was not an easy job to be had just by anyone!

I have looked into the eye of a panda on a eucalyptus tree in China, and I have held the special female coconut in my hands at Pralin. Coco de mer fruits are among the largest of coconuts. They take about twenty-five years to ripen. The male and the female varieties are easily visible hanging from the trees. To establish the sexual identity does not need any imagination, and the preponderant male qualities will put the best of stallions to shame. I found it exciting that they have the ability to mate in distant trees despite their fixed positions. I liked the idea of their being able to somehow sway in the wind to come closer at times to fondle the hair of the partner. I could hear her whispering as the wind passed between the leaves, as if she were expressing her satisfaction and pride of having successfully conceived this new flower—a newborn soon to be bestowed with refreshing water inside a tender wall of energized vitality. A hardened shell of smooth green exterior will quickly envelop and guard this child of the wind through its long journey along the wavy contour of the salty Indian Ocean. It will converse with the fish. It will hug the white sands of the shores of Africa. It will greet its long-lost relatives along this massive Gondwanaland that moved away, taking its family to distant places.

It is eager to share the sounds of the inner splashing of the sweet water while riding the waves of the engulfing ocean. As it floats along the seesaw of this bouncy highway, it still maintains its pride of its heritage. It is gifted to impart curiosity of its hidden source of energy to all who get to touch it and taste it.

I have seen a malamute chase a squirrel up a tree, the wisteria shed a flower in excitement, and the pear tree being all shook up but pleased by the effort, rewarded the frustrated dog with a substitute, an offering of its own fruit. I read about Dr. Wister from Philadelphia who named this flower that reminds me of beautiful hanging earrings. I have picked it as a gift for my girl.

I have seen Secretariat run so fast that the whole television screen was empty behind him. It reminded me of the time when someone told me that they had such a small television that only "Tora" of *Tora, Tora, Tora* could be seen. But I had a big screen when I watched that Derby. I have listened to Bing Crosby sing "White Christmas," and the surrounding silence was so embalming that I could actually hear the sound of the snow falling on the grass beneath me.

I have remembered reading *Kubla Khan* with my grandfather:

A savage place! As holy and enchanted
As e'er beneath a waning moon was haunted
By woman wailing for her demon-lover!

I have flown a balloon and skimmed the treetops. I have scraped the waters of Ohio and then taken off to almost five thousand feet with a "pss-pss" of propane. I have allowed myself to be blown away until my gas almost ran out. I have driven a Maserati on the expressway while dreaming of Richard Petty in the Indianapolis 500. I made it to my destination, but I was successful in confusing the policeman at my talent and lack of intelligence both at the same time.

I have seen the mamba of Africa and the cobra of India. I have even seen a snake eating a rat.

I enjoyed hiking in the Smokies and bathing in the Monongahela River. I learned to chew Mail Pouch while I canoed in the rivers of Kentucky. My excitement spilled me over once when I rafted down the New River in West Virginia as I was practicing the new chew. I remember the time I fell over when I swallowed the juice of these brown pungent leaves. I was less than knowledgeable of the techniques of disposal of the brown juice during the initial stages. However, as I progressed from being a novice to an expert, I have acquired the talent of expelling this aromatic fluid to a significant distance. Now I have developed the strength in my buccal muscles necessary to produce the characteristic sound that is necessary for graduation to the higher level.

I have seen a male ostrich, all decked out in his colorful plume, chase his female counterpart for miles not knowing that honey is made in the comforts of a comb, in a state of complete contentment. It didn't know that it is the female initiative that curls the plume, raises the legs, and creates the situation where it would be lifted forever. I suppose that he has not learned the techniques of having the female attracted to him so that he won't have to run on the prairies all day looking for a "chick" to make the wholesome and uplifting union.

Often I lie in the meadows and admire the thorough-breds, particularly the new foals with their slender props and smooth joints as they chew the bluegrass. I believe they imagine themselves running down the track at Churchill Downs on that special first Saturday of May. I have seen them running to their mother for that necessary reassurance—"Am I good enough? "Are those markings as good as my dad's?" Soon I would hear a loving and approving "nee-hee" and then a practice gallop to the white fence.

The dandelions are thrilled to be included in this in crowd, and they give the horses a reward by swaying and singing from our very own Ronnie Milsap, "you can't get rid of me, darling." But one day only one of these horses will mature to get that special rose wreath in May.

I have driven a boat while my children learned waterskiing in our lakes. I have admired my son driving the tractor in the field like it was a tank. He played imaginary war games while the steering handle came off and he had to resort to primitive warfare techniques of using it as a shield.

I have treated my family to a meal of rabbits that I shot with a .22 rifle in our backyard. I have stayed up all night to cook a pig on a spit to celebrate Lamb's essay on "Roasting a Pig." During the preparation of this gastronomic delicacy, I have often passed on to a state of slumber with a beer can in my hand and my feet next to the fire. I have been awakened by my son in a state of confusion, with smoking shoes and many warm toes.

I have prayed with my children—"Remember not the sins of my youth, nor my transgressions, according to thy mercy remember thou me for thy goodness sake, O Lord" (Psalm 25:7). My son once flattered me when he was eight years old. We were working all day in the field together, shoveling manure from the barn, and we had just sat down to reflect while having a Coke or a beer. I do not remember exactly what we were talking about. He looked up to me and said, "Dad, there is nothing left for me to do when I grow up. You have done even a pig roast." I remember that moment vividly, and prayed. Secretly, I hoped that he would not grow up and I would remain his hero all the time. But I knew better. I convinced myself to be happy at a later date when he would be twenty-five so that I would suddenly appear smarter in his eyes again. That day I gave him more than twenty-five cents for helping me with the yard work. I made him think that it was for extra hard work, but in reality I knew that it was a bribe for telling me that I was great!

I often told my children that I did not know how to be a dad because I had no formal schooling on the subject. I tried to prepare information in history, geography, and plain old boring stuff. They knew about the highest mountain and the Mariana trench.

They learned that samurai were members of the Japanese warrior class that rose to power in the twelfth century. They had an unwritten code of conduct, which held bravery, honor, and personal loyalty above life itself. Ritual suicide by seppuku (disembowelment) was considered a respectable alternative to capture or defeat.

We talked about Jhansi-ki-Rani (the queen of Jhansi), a

brave Rajput woman who jumped from a fort with her horse to kill herself rather than be captured by the British. I remembered a story Dr. Hunt told me about the penguins. A little boy wanted to know about the penguins and expressed his desire as such. His mother was busy and suggested that he ask his father about them because he did not appear to be busy at that time. The little boy quipped that he did not want to know that much about penguins. I thought this was a great lesson I received from my professor. I tried to keep the information periods short with my children.

One time we were watching the Indianapolis 500, and Budweiser had its float pulled by the Clydesdale horses. We talked about these horses, which came to America in the mid-1800s, and the fact that this heavy draft-horse breed originated in Lanarkshire, Scotland, near the River Clyde. A Flemish stallion improved the breed by mating with the local mares.

We had a horse named Stockton and two donkeys, Jack and Jill. I gave Jill away to a friend because his cows were having a difficult time finding the water hole and Jill was really good at it. It seemed that shortly after that, Jack was trying to mount the horse. Having never had this experience, Stockton was quite confused at this dilemma. He started kicking the donkey rather vigorously whenever this animal of lower caste made any amorous posturing. I personally was proud of the choice the donkey made, but I believe the stallion had some say in it as well! We enjoyed watching them running in circles in the field, I believe, as an alternative, to burn the pent-up energy.

I have climbed Kalapatthar and admired the beautiful Mt. Everest at its glory. I have inhaled the spirit of rejuvenation from the virgin snow on the lofty peaks of the surrounding mountains. I have looked at the mighty Khumbha Glacier and imagined the secrets that it has buried in its cool enclave. I have watched the "calving" of the glaciers at Glacier Bay and shared the thrill of those kayaking in the frosty bay waters.

As my lover lay on my lap at the Red River Gorge, I read, "Men may come and men may go, but I go on for ever" from Alfred, Lord Tennyson's "Song from the Brook." We sipped Dom Perignon from swan flutes and tasted gross grain beluga while I glanced at the long ash of my Cohiba cigar lying by its mate in the smooth valley of the ashtray, wishing to be stoked and rekindled again.

A jug of wine, a Loaf of Bread—and Thou
Beside me singing in the Wilderness—
Oh, Wilderness were Paradise enow!

I believe "for all have sinned, and come short of the Glory of God" and in spite of my little peccadilloes, "God so loved the world that He gave His Son, that whoever believes in Him shall not perish but have eternal life" (John 3:16).

• • • • •

As a young intern, I came with a desire to make something of myself without any help from the family. This was difficult for me at first.

I often felt the need to talk to someone who knew a little more about life than I did. I, of course, knew nothing. I was quite lonesome. However, I soon made friends with other interns and residents. Many of them thought that they knew a lot, but there were others who loved me for my ignorance. I have remained a friend with the latter.

I stood at the Los Angeles airport outside the gate trying to decide what I should do now. I had just arrived from Manila after being at the Manila Hilton where some woman had offered to bathe me. I did not think that was a good idea, particularly because she wanted to charge me fifty dollars for a task that I could accomplish by myself without any help. I had also been to Saigon and Tokyo prior to coming to the United States. I have forgotten now, but I remember distinctly that in one restaurant they offered monkey brains. I had the option of choosing my monkey in the back room, much like one chooses lobsters from an aquarium.

Well, now I was in another country—my final destination, a place where I was going to find my identity and establish myself as an individual. This is where individual rights are honored and a person has the freedom to pursue his or her goal in life. Many years ago, I had read "What Then Is An American" by Crevecoeur.

> He is an American, who, leaving behind him all his ancient prejudices and manners, receives new ones from the new mode of life he has embraced, the new government he obeys, and the new rank he holds. He becomes an American by being received in the broad lap of our great Alma Mater.

This had kindled a fire in me. This is the sweet land of liberty.

I was coming from a great culture where many children from America came to find themselves away from their parents. I did not know exactly how many found themselves or truly became scholars in Indian philosophy, but many certainly enjoyed the flavors of cannabis during the process. It is a land where Sri Ramakrishna said, "I have practiced all religions: Hinduism, Islam, Christianity, and I have also followed the paths of the different Hindu sects—I have found that it is the same God toward whom all are directing their steps, though along different paths. You must try all beliefs and traverse all the different ways once." It is here that Rabindranath Tagore wrote in "Gitanjali," "That I should make much of myself and turn it on all sides, thus casting colored shadows on thy radiance—such is thy Maya." I remember reading but not understanding, "Thou settest a barrier in thine own being and then callest thy severed self in myriad notes. This thy self-separation has taken body in me."

These concepts did not come to me until many years later. It is believed that God created different forms of his body and illusions to keep the evil away. There is a tremendous similarity between Christ breaking bread and saying, "This is my body," with this concept of Hinduism where God has given pieces of his body for all mankind. There is a merging. There is a unity despite having different forms or names. There is harmony in the soul and communion with God.

· · · · ·

America was involved in the Vietnam War, and I knew just barely enough to talk about it. I did not understand the politics behind it then, and I am not sure I do even now. The young generation was still panting with Elvis, singing with the Beatles who were passing on the spirit they imbibed from their acquaintance with the Maharishi. The younger generation was floating with the advice of Timothy Leary of getting it up and getting it on or more precisely "tune in, turn on, and drop out."

I saw the mass of men and immediately tried to understand the meaning of "leading a life of quiet desperation." I am used to seeing masses of men that move constantly, but then they sit down for a cup of tea or just move on to somewhere else to move again. There was something different about this place. They were dressed well, and there was an air of business around them. No one greeted or smiled but just moved on.

I walked outside the airport building and stood on an overpass and saw a display of moving cars, a scene that I had only experienced in movies. I wondered why everyone drove so fast and so close to each other, a question that still puzzles me. I had noticed earlier that everyone had stood up as soon as the pilot had turned off the seat belt light. I found everyone standing in the aisle for a long time instead of sitting down in the seats before anyone actually got off the plane. It seemed there was urgency in the air to do something or go somewhere, but I could not figure out to do what and to go where.

I had a ten-hour layover. My luggage was checked and I had nothing to do but think. Therefore, I went to the best place of meditation that I knew in those days. I drank six martinis and boarded the plane to Louisville. The first time I heard anything important was when the stewardess made some announcement that we were going to land at Kansas City. I was not used to this type of English pronunciation, and I had to ask her to repeat. I wanted to know if I needed to get out or just allow my spirit to rest for the next couple of hours. She thought I had a cute accent. I was pleased with my confidence. I wanted my first encounter with the instructor in Louisville to be at a level of consciousness that is considered normal for a standard medical interview.

The plane landed in a small airport. I felt comfortable. I took a taxi from the airport to arrive at my designated hospital. The taxi cost me three dollars in those days. I was excited because I knew that my career was going to begin now. I forgot that it had actually begun almost ten years before when I graduated from high school.

I recall meeting the receptionist at the entrance of the hospital, who pointed me to a seat while she paged someone. She had a large bird's-nest coiffure on top of her head and wore too much makeup. I immediately knew she had something to hide. Later, I got to know her a little better and I was glad she had the capacity to hide unnecessary elements of life. Very shortly, she called me by moving her pointing finger back and forth at the metacarpophalangeal joint. It is the same joint motion that occurs when we give the bird, but a different finger. As I found out later, she was indeed quite dexterous. I responded like a puppy dog and left the lobby to meet my new acquaintances, some of whom became close friends.

After I had a meeting with the director of the training program, I was introduced to different floors by one of my colleagues. Then it was lunchtime, where I met the rest of the crew, and soon I was introduced to a poker game.

I also met a man who carried a radio in his pocket and always listened to the horse races all around the country all day. It seemed to me that the induction into the poker hall of fame in the interns' quarters meant that they decided I could afford to lose. It was an interesting game where no one lost much because nobody had much to lose. It was assumed that the fellow who was winning would go across the street when he passed his cards and buy White Castle hamburgers. These cost only six cents a piece.

Those days were great for most of us, gastronomically speaking, that is. We could literally eat twenty of those delicious miniburgers soaked in lard and never get sick. It should be known that we were not a boring bunch of poker players. We played a variety of games, including blackjack, and on many occasions the game lasted all night.

It was not at all unusual for some of the staff ob-gyn doctors to spend the night with us after having come to the hospital to deliver babies who decided to wait to be born. This type of insensitivity caused them frustration, and the situation was felt to be more aggravating because the doctor had a sleepless night. I don't know if it's true, but I heard that the fear of litigation from distressed babies or their parents subsequently led these doctors to schedule C-sections at more convenient times. It was our loss, because those were the guys who had the money

I still vividly remember the first night I was on duty. I went to the pediatric floor early in the afternoon to see which nurse was going to be working with me and if she would help without embarrassing me in case I was called to an emergency. This fear was so genuine that I made sure that one of my friends would take the call with me that evening. Despite my going to a fine medical school, I had this fear, and when I talked with others, they shared the same feeling, except that they were more reserved and not so vocal.

I had prayed for a nonemergency night, and God listened to me. He got me involved with a child who had the croup, and I, the inexperienced, became experienced that night with the help of a fine pediatric nurse! Little did I know how many intravenous lines I would be starting on baby's heads for the rest of my life.

As soon as I became comfortable, I realized that we could not work for only four dollars an hour in the emergency room. This was the going rate, and all of us needed the extra work to pay for some incidentals, such as going out on a date or a little extra for the poker game. I organized a strike by the interns to the consternation of the director. He was an understanding man, and we were able to convince him of our need. We started working for eight dollars an hour. An acceptable resolution for a difficult proposition!

The internship and a year of general surgery at Louisville were extremely helpful in preparation for my future. I met Dr. R. Roth, who took a personal interest in me and taught me neurology. He was the busiest neurologist in those days. He understood my interest and urgency. He took time out for me at ten at night and demonstrated neurological signs and also the science and art of reading the electroencephalograph (EEG). I had a difficult time at first figuring out how someone could read and dictate fifteen EEGs in a two-hour time limit, particularly as each was almost an inch and a half thick.

Dr. M. Colbert was a fine orthopaedic surgeon who taught me how country doctors work. He was a fine technician and a soft-spoken man who fixed broken bones, casted twisted limbs, and served the people with a distinctive flair all his own. He used scarlet red on everything when it was popular. I recall using it on my horse's leg as well when it sustained an injury to its leg by jumping over a barbed-wire fence.

I remember talking to Dr. Giannini during a plastic surgery procedure about my then pecuniary obligations and that I had a date and I felt strapped.

He was kind enough to give me a tip on one of his horses that ran at Churchill Downs. I was pleased with the outcome that day.

It took me many years, and only when I owned a few race horses, to realize that the owner actually does not know if his horse is going to win. The feeling of knowledge is imparted on the owner by others who ask questions about the possibility of the owner's horse winning on a certain day. I somehow believed for a while that I was empowered with such knowledge. I had to try hard to tell myself not to believe in that false perception when I became an owner. I had to recognize that I did not know any more about horses then than when I was just a simple loser at the betting window.

My trainer educated me the most one day when my horse was getting ready to run. The odds were 20-1 on the tote board. Jennie was always very optimistic. She told me not to worry, because the horse could not read. Therefore, it was not going to feel insulted by the racing fans for their lack of faith in its ability. I had hoped to win that day and was quite disappointed by the skeptical odds. Secretly, I had hired a fortune-teller. She had informed me that the horse was going to win. I did not believe the fortune-teller until I saw the ticket in her hand with the number of my horse.

The trumpet blew, and my horse walked gallantly in front of everyone with pride and dignity. I heard, "And they are off." I watched on the big screen, and I could hear the sound of the galloping hooves as they went past the sixth furlong post. It came from behind. The jockey was kneeling on top of it and whipping its hindquarter with a mean stick. I saw its sweaty, muscular body whipping past the seventh furlong post. It gave its last gas spurt in full gallop as smoke belched through its nostrils. It came through the finish line in third position.

I was disappointed at the fortune-teller. She told me that I lacked faith in her abilities. This was my first encounter with a person who claimed to be clairvoyant. She felt slighted that I had called her a fortune-teller. She claimed to have told Nancy Reagan that her husband would lose all memory of the Iran-Contra affair, and, therefore, there was nothing to worry about.

There was a steward's enquiry because my jockey said that at the fourth furlong marker the first two horses had bumped my Jet Did It. I could not believe it. They moved number 9 into the first position, and my fortune-teller and I went home happy. I never hired the fortune-teller again because I didn't want her to be wrong, but I became a believer in her power to predict. I often wondered, though, why she hadn't taken advantage of this talent to promote herself a little more. It didn't appear to me that she was promoting Versace through her wardrobe. Maybe she was just a local girl and liked Kmart.

I had known that in America we could benefit from all our talents, even those that are not apparent. Stacked lumber fell on a customer's head while shopping in a Home Depot in Ft. Lauderdale, Florida. She claimed that the mild head injury robbed her of a supernatural power: her ability to go on "automatic" to undergo pain-free surgery without anesthesia. The Broward circuit court jury awarded her $5,000 and her husband $1,000 for loss of her services. Judge P. L. Marko agonized before letting the juries even consider awarding money for paranormal damages. He said after the verdict, "There is no legal precedent for either allowing it or denying it" (*Houston Chronicle,* February 1991). I assumed that the husband's award was owing to failure in his wife's debriefing capabilities.

• • • • •

During my internship in Louisville, I had the opportunity to work with several physicians. Dr. H. Asman was a rectal surgeon. His name was interesting to me because it seemed like the caste system in India, where people had names according to their profession. He informed me that was not the case in America, although his patients remember him more easily.

I have never seen anyone perform a better hemorrhoid operation than the way he did. Patients had very little complaint and no one needed dilatation or such. His patients went home on the second postoperative day. They, of course, continued their warm sitz baths while watching television. Many patients complained that our hospital bathroom did not have television, and one person confided in me that watching "Gunsmoke" was a pleasing distraction for him while he bathed his behind in a bathtub. Some others liked the girls in the "Lawrence Welk Show" during their time of painting warm poultice to the bottom. People felt comfortable talking to me. I was the "Oh" doctor. In those days, when the attending doctor made rounds with his entourage, the most junior intern was at the back end of the trail of the senior doctors who made decisions and discussed the patients in the early mornings. The patients would usually wake up just about the time everyone's back was turned and they were getting ready to leave. So, when the patient would ask a question with the exclamation and salutation "Oh, doctor," I would be at the back end of the line and turn around.

During this period of my training, Dr. J. Hemmer was a general surgeon who took it upon himself to educate me. I scrubbed with him on many gallbladder operations, bypasses for vascular disease of the lower limbs, colostomies, hysterectomies, and other surgeries. He was a meticulous surgeon, and his manners were impeccable. He gave me more responsibilities as I made progress. On one occasion, Dr. Hemmer asked me to remove the sutures from the leg of a priest (our patient) and write a necessary prescription for him while Dr. Hemmer was out of town. After I carried out my task, this Canadian Jesuit priest gave me a dollar and with utmost love said, "You will make many of these in your life, but this has the blessing of an eighty-year-old man." I still have the dollar and cherish the memory. I have always felt that the priest was like the bishop in *Les Miserables* who had placed a blanket of blessing in my soul! This love that he shared is so personal to me that I did not want anybody to know about it for many years. I felt like Joseph, as though this blessing did not belong to me and I was afraid that I might lose it.

All these men in Louisville taught me in a didactic manner as well as demonstrating in their personality the essential qualities of a surgeon. They exemplified patience, persistence, perseverance, and compassion for their patients. I was introduced to true American medicine.

• • • • •

I had learned to play poker as a child, when I was twelve years or so. My father had his friends over to our house every Saturday for a card game that I was not allowed to watch. However, about twenty feet outside the window was a wall about two feet wide separating our property from that of the neighbor. I usually sat on this wall during the game until I felt that I had learned the game.

After I was sixteen, I was allowed to participate in the game with my dad's money. My dad thought that I had keen eyes and persistence. I recall a time in that period when I would tell the bus conductor that I had misplaced the bus money, and, thus, I would travel free, thanks to the conductor. I walked home from school to save the return money as well. Almost every evening, I would gamble with that money with the neighbor's son who also had acquired a similar talent. Alas! The trick was soon discovered. One of the bus conductors happened to have been my father's patient, and saw me in his dispensary. We had to forgo our gambling habits at the young age of twelve as my behavior was considered despicable and unbecoming of a doctor's son. But I knew that it was like learning to ride a bicycle: it would come back to me when I needed to be part of the gang again.

I stayed with my dad only for a short period after my grandfather died, then went away to a school on top of a fort in Gwalior about a thousand miles away from home. The government of India provided one hundred soldiers to live on the fort and protect the children from being kidnapped. Kidnapping was very prevalent in those days in that particular part of the country. Moreover, the prince of Gwalior was going to school with us. I really did not go to any real school where there was any structured program prior to this. The British had just been removed from the country. This was a school where children were being prepared to govern the distressed and oppressed India. This is where we learned to be citizens of India and not of an exploited colony.

This is where the future spirit of India would be marinated with tolerance, sautéed with humility, and garnished with a business sense to improve India from within, such that one day all the oppression of two hundred years would be forgotten to a new, glorious future. Indians do not bear grudges for the past maltreatment, but they had to learn that their pride had to be rekindled and that they had to rise to a new consciousness. We could not sit on the merits of the past and the gold and the jewelry that we had for centuries. We knew that we were special because we were plundered over the centuries. We knew of Alexander the Great, the Persians, the Mongols, the Portuguese, and, of course, the British. The British philanderers left our country most destitute. Our workers could make Muslim silk saris that would fit inside matchboxes. Our *pusmin* (hair of the mountain goats) shoulder wraps could pass through a ring. But people in India could not afford them, and they were being sold in Manchester for foreigners to enjoy. We had the Taj Mahal, but Shajahan's jewelry was in the British

Museum near the London Bridge. Mr. A. Yale had accumulated a lot of wealth while being in India. Attorneys for Warren Hastings's (governor general of Bengal, 1772–1785) were arguing that the laws of the West should not apply to the East. It was perfectly fine to spend less money for the education in the whole state of West Bengal than in the city of London. We learned that Queen Isabella sent Columbus to visit India to get spices. Columbus's erroneous course led to the discovery of the Americas. We were saved from another plundering.

We read about the Boston Tea Party and the agony of the people of another colony who wanted the people represented in government. Here, we were taught that all colonies would fail one day, because power sharing is the fair rule and fairness would always prevail over unkindness.

I read about the lives of Vivekananda and Sister Nivedita. I imagined his speech in the Chicago meeting of the Parliament of Religions in 1893. I imagined that the vast audience of Americans must have been enthralled by the depth of his voice and his conviction in explaining his religious beliefs. They must have been surprised to have seen a well-built, muscular, educated man as a representative from a country of beggars, as the British would have them believe.

We sat every evening to meditate facing the West (sunset) looking at a statue of Gandhi in his famous Dandee walk (when he walked across the nation carrying a stick).

I learned about Edmund Burke, the great orator who was elected a member of Parliament in Bristol. He became a hero of mine after I read some of his writings. He spent most of his energy investigating the British East India Company, which exploited and repressed India to the fullest. Burke successfully impeached Warren Hastings in 1787, but eventually Hastings was acquitted. I was delighted to find a copy of his original speeches and present it to my niece who is a barrister in Birmingham.

We played sports such as cricket, hockey, and soccer. We participated in debate and elocution. We went on bicycle trips and rode horses and participated in gymnastics and physical training classes. I was not much for the PT classes and often made fun of the teacher. Our classes were small, and we knew each other and lived in the dormitories. We had a substitute teacher once who entered the class and shouted, "Order, order!" One of the students yelled back, "Double whiskey and soda." He had to go to the principal.

Our school doctor was not too excited about our illnesses or us. I remember I was having a stomachache, and he told the nurse to paint some Tinc. of Iodine on my stomach. The nurse actually carried out this task. It humiliated me. I was insulted because it stopped my deception prior to having reached its goal. I knew even then that stomachache deserved a more serious investigation in the hospital! Not only did it not help me to stay away from the school, it even stained my clean white shirt. Our principal was extremely kind to us. I was once in the sick room for a few days because of an "I could not see" type symptom. The nurse had complained to the principal that she had noticed my shadow in the window of her room when she was changing her clothes. However, the principal explained to her that I could not see, and, therefore, she should not worry. I do not remember what I saw anyway!

We sang our national anthem, which Rabindranath Tagore had written when he was asked to write something for the salutation to Lord Mountbatten.

One of his famous poems that we read every day,

"Sanchayita," was written on our wall.

> Where the mind is without fear
> And the head is held high;
> Where the mind is led forward by thee
> Into ever widening thoughts and action;
> Into that heaven of freedom
> My father let my country awake.

After my mother died when I was about six months old, her father raised me in his home and kept his promise to my mother. I was not expected. My mother had tuberculosis when she carried me, and she was asked to have an abortion. However, she chose to have me and died instead. I did not know all this until I was sixteen. I wanted to go back inside my mother's womb when I learned all this, but she wasn't there. I did not have any-body to talk to about my feelings, so I just kept quiet. I certainly did not feel like talking to my sister or my brother, who would have thought that I killed their mother. This was a difficult time for me not to have anyone to confide in, although there was nothing to talk about. So I did a lot of what most adolescents do in the bathroom. One of the kids from my class told me that I was going to be blind. He said that he had learned that from his friends. Now I wear glasses, and he is still my friend.

My father treated me OK. He told me about my birth because I insisted on knowing what happened to my mom. My father drank a lot of whiskey, and always the finest scotch available. He gave me a shot of whiskey and then explained to me what happened. He confided in me my mom's wish. He also told me that streptomycin (antibiotic for treatment of tuberculosis) became available in India six months after she died from tubercular peritonitis (water in the abdomen). He chose not to get remarried because he was concerned that the new wife might not love his children. Moreover, he was a successful doctor and he thought that the marriage might end up being of monetary interest to the woman. He was also not willing to start a new family.

He loved me the way he knew best. He took me fishing as often as he went. He taught me to gamble at the races and gave me a gift of a bottle of Black Label Johnny Walker and a pack of 555 cigarettes on my sixteenth birthday. He told me not to smoke or drink the cheap stuff if I could not afford the good kind. He taught me what the good kinds were in those days. He had loved my mother very much. He never spoke about her, and if I asked, he would skirt the issue because he did not like to be tearful. However, every November he would place flowers next to my mom's picture that he had in his room until the day he died—well, at least until the last time I saw him. November was the month my mother was born. He always celebrated that.

He was a loving man, but never spoke much about it. However, his every gesture was full of love and compassion. He was proud of our heritage. He knew the names of the male members of seven generations before him. He knew about most of them. He had the details written in a notebook. He reminded me that I was an important person of the eighth generation, and that people would look at me in the future in a way similar to the way we were reading about our predecessors. He talked about the fact that a good tree bears good fruit, and I congratulated him for being a good tree. He reminded me of the importance of pedigree. He talked about good breeding and about the gene pool in successive generations. I wondered, at times, if my dad was talking about horses or us, particularly because I knew about his interest and knowledge in horse racing. He quoted George Santayana: "Those who can not remember the past are condemned to repeat it." I read parts of "The Sense of Beauty" and the "Interpretations of Poetry and Religion." This was difficult for me to understand and did not make a lot of sense, despite the fact that I liked to read Robert Browning. I told him that I liked Elizabeth Browning a lot more because her loving poems seemed so endearing to her husband. On the other hand, Robert had a fierceness about him. We talked about abstract philosophy. Santayana's concept of aesthetic feelings being transitory and to judge that anything is beautiful is "virtually to establish an ideal" gave us substance for argument at times. My father told me that when I quoted someone, I should describe their thoughts using a different word than what they used in their original writing. He thought plagiarism improper, and said I should always give credit to the authors for their thoughts and then I should try to think on my own. I did not know sometimes whether I was thinking on my own or if I was just being a parrot.

He mentioned about the famous family of Marie and Pierre Curie who isolated polonium in July 1898 and radium in December 1898. They received the Nobel Prize in 1903. Marie received a second Nobel Prize in 1911 for her work in chemistry. Marie's daughter, Irene, and son-in-law, Frederick, also received a Nobel Prize in 1935 for their work in chemistry as well. He admired famous families.

He was a man of passion. We often read Robert Frost together, and he particularly liked this passage from "The Road Not Taken":

> I shall be telling this with a sigh
> Somewhere ages and ages hence:

Two roads diverged in a wood, and I—
I took the one less traveled by
And that has made all the difference.

He did not believe what Plato said about being chained to the wall in a prison in a cave with fire burning on our backs. I did not believe that we are just looking at shadows, and the light outside is blinding.

We talked about the fact that it is possible that retribution is predetermined, and we will receive what is due for the things done while in the body, whether good or bad (2 Cor 5:10).

We discussed Coleridge, and about the theme of "The Rime of the Ancient Mariner." I learned the story of this mariner who was trapped in guilt from committing a crime against the principles of life. He had killed an innocent albatross. He perceived the presence of hell while alive. We looked at the pictures of the paintings by famous Indian artists as well as by artists of other countries. Botticelli's Mystic Nativity comes to mind, where there is depiction of devils fleeing underground to hell and the winding path on earth leading to Christ recalling the imagery of Dante's *Divine Comedy*. My father thought death was in reality an escape from punishment, and, therefore, he did not approve of capital punishment. He thought that condemning someone to a life of guilt was much worse. He said that some people never felt guilty because of their psychosocial development.

Sometimes we talked about making scientific connections to the philosophical aspects of life. In such situations, he often gave me examples of Sir Isaac Newton's theory that every action has an opposite reaction and the fact that there are consequences to every choice we make. We talked about Byron and Shelley and we read Alaster and discussed the solitary pursuit of an ideal love. My dad truly loved. He did not accept atheism, and he thought even that was risky. He said he always believed that a divine force guided him. He often said to me that his patients got well many times even when he really didn't do anything. He was a strong believer in the power of prayer. Without faith, it was like handling a boat in a rough sea all by oneself. He believed in "For unto whomsoever much is given, of him shall be much required" (Luke 12:48). I was happy that he told me that he would give everything away to those who he thought would need it the most.

He read poetry and wrote the most beautiful Bengali lyrics and often read them to me. He knew how to cook well and always ate very well. He believed in living and going forward. He drew pictures and cartoons and sketches. Almost all his children patients got a sample of a sketch by the time they came out of the room after an injection or such. It was often a monkey or an elephant or a giraffe drawn on his prescription pad.

He taught me to trust. I remember once my brother asked him for a substantial sum of money while studying in college. My brother had written him a letter, and this monetary request was in very small letters at the end of the letter. My father assumed that the expense was for the pipettes (tubes that are used in the chemistry class) rather than for the Fallopian tubes (tubes attached to the ovary). My father always was proud of whatever we wrote, and shared our writings with his friends who were his poker buddies. I recall one of them telling him to find out the cause for my brother's need. My father told him that he would rather not ask because if it were not a reasonable cause, he did not want to hear a lie from his son.

He worked long hours and was exceptionally disciplined. He left home at four-thirty in the morning with a small bag in his hand. After he swam for an hour in the River Ganges, he walked through the market with his bag filled with meat, fish, vegetables, and whatever else he needed. There was rarely any exchange of money. He often told me that money makes our hand dirty. It took me many years to understand the deeper meaning of that statement. Almost all these merchants were my father's patients, and Dad treated them for free and often gave them medications that they could not afford.

Even as an adult, very few people actually knew my name and almost everyone addressed me as Daaktarbabu's son. I used to sit in our living room when he returned. The room was full of patients. He would greet them and then sit down without his shirt next to the windowsill where he would shave. There was always someone who read the headlines of the newspaper to him because he did not have time. He would examine patients with soap on his cheeks and the stethoscope in his ears, and at times the pen replaced the razor in his right hand while he wrote a prescription. The young man kept on reading through all this because my dad probably paid for his college, and this was his way of paying off my dad. When my wife, an American woman, visited him the first time, she did not know who lived in the house and who did not. I believe one has to experience it to believe it. Through all this, Dad gave instructions to the cook, and breakfast would be served while Dad went in the house for a shower and a change of clothes. Our water was stored in buckets those days, and one had to pour the water on the head with a small tumbler or such. We called it a hand shower. This is very much the way English people take a bath in the bathtub these days. I believe the strong shower is an American concept.

The chauffeur would have the car ready, and everyone who was present at that moment would join Dad for breakfast.

He always ate eggs, fruits, and bread, and juice from a fibrous fruit called bel. He thought fresh fruits were essential for staying healthy and regular.

Whenever I was home from school, I went to see the patients with him. Essentially, what this meant was that I traveled with him all day in his car while he stopped periodically to make home visits. He would discuss with me Sanskrit poetry and talk about politics and express his opinion about some of the world leaders. He told me about Hermann Collitz, who taught Sanskrit and comparative linguistics at the University of Halle before moving to the United States. Now this name has become better known to me since my daughter received a degree in Greek and Latin from Bryn Mawr college where he was a professor in 1886. Among many of his publications, he had published *Collection of Greek Dialect Inscriptions,* which proved to be a major contribution to Greek comparative linguistics. We often talked about literature because he was an avid reader and enjoyed reading just about everything. He challenged me to memorize a thirty-page book of Jaydev's poetry written in Sanskrit and offered me one hundred rupees as an incentive. I won the bet!

He told me to read about the caduceus. It stems from the Greek word *karykeion* and describes a staff surmounted by two wings around which two serpents are entwined with their heads facing each other. It was originally a herald's wand and a symbol of peace commonly associated with the Greek god Hermes. In early Babylonian history, the caduceus itself was a god and not merely an emblem.

The caduceus is seen on Babylonian cylinders and on the libation vase of King Gudea, about 3500 B.C. The two entwined serpents, perhaps male and female, represented at that time gods Ningishizida and Ishtar. Ishtar was the personification of productivity and fertility.

He liked mythology. We had a constant exchange of ideas and an enthusiastic encouragement in regard to the ways of life. He discussed Oedipus and Jean Cocteau's interpretation of the theme in *The Infernal Machine*. I remember that he told me about Prometheus, who was punished by being chained on top of a mountain for bringing the knowledge of fire to humans from the gods. He told me that although the vultures came and ate his liver everyday, it grew back very rapidly, signifying the fact that people even then had the knowledge of the regenerative power of the liver. We talked about the Indus Valley civilization and how every river of importance had an older civilization associated with it. We talked about the Tigris and Euphrates Rivers and about the flowers of Basra. He mentioned to me that Shiva is the Hindu god of creation and destruction, and women often touch and lick or kiss the lingam (the phallic symbol) to gain his enlivening spirit for their husbands. These were days long before Viagra was available in the market. The bull was considered his mascot, and, as time went on, people worshipped the bull as a symbolic gesture to honor Shiva.

While traveling in his car as well as just before his nap in the afternoon, he would read Harold Robbins, Agatha Christie, Peter Cheyney, that is, mostly the stuff that did not require much thinking. I recall that he had asked me not to read his copy of *Lady Chatterley's Lover*. I was only twelve or thirteen years old then, and he thought I was not in a position to comprehend the depth of sexual intimacy. He did not like me to look at the pictures of Kama-Sutra as well but I liked them. We did not have *Playboy* magazine then, or at least I did not know about it. When I saw the magazine later after coming to the United States, the pictures of naked women did not seem as exciting as they did when I was younger. I felt sad and worried, thinking that maybe when I understand sex at last it may turn out to be not interesting. I overcame that fear. It was apparent to me at an early age that somehow I always did exactly opposite of what my father would ask me to do.

He knew about Sir Alexander Edmund Cockburn, who defined obscenity. In his legal definition, he stated the test of obscenity as ". . . whether the tendency of the matter charged as obscenity is to deprave and corrupt those whose minds are open to such influences, and into whose hands a publication of this sort may fall." His tolerance was remarkable. He paddled me only once, when I was verbally abusive to his friend's son outside the house in a manner that was audible to the entire neighborhood.

• • • • •

We would arrive at the dispensary around eleven in the morning, and he always was late for his patients. Most patients took a number like in an ice cream shop and either sat or stood as the "Daaktarbabu" examined his patients. He felt their abdomen, looked in their eyes, checked their tongue, and checked their blood pressure. He talked while doing all this, and wrote prescriptions, and sometimes gave advice on family matters. He was a true friend to most of his patients. I sat and observed.

He had a back room for examining women, and sometimes he used the room to look at slides for malaria and the stool specimens. He often told me about the spleen, and I learned a lot about worms at an early age. I remember him yelling at one of his patients who brought a large clay container full of stool and placed it on his table because he was told to bring a specimen. I remember the patient told the doctor that he could not decide which part he should choose because there was a lot of variety. That was the first time I learned about roundworm and whipworm—right there. He taught me about anemia and hookworm, and he treated many patients with malaria. Quinine and chloroquine were the two medicines available in those days for treating malaria. He saw patients who sometimes had jumping of the legs at night, and he treated that condition with quinine as well. Unfortunately, we still do not know how to treat jumping leg syndrome. He did not know how it worked, but they did not call him anymore because they could sleep through the night. My dad did not like to be called in the night.

He told me that the fields of neurology, cardiology, and geriatrics would develop the most in the future because as we live longer, the above two systems would be most affected.

He was an outstanding clinician; this became a lot more apparent to me when I became a doctor. He was able to distinguish between kala-azar and the typhoid spleen by palpation, and I heard him talk about dengue fever and the amoebic liver. Nowadays, patients are treated so early that I believe the books have to be revised because the antibiotics cure the patients before there is a chance for the milliary rash of typhoid fever to develop or for the spleen to enlarge.

He had a degree in tropical medicine and in public health as well. He often talked to me about leprosy and plague. He introduced me to Bocaccio and the plague in Europe.

He often expressed frustration that several medications that were available in the West were not easily accessible to him because of the cost constraints. He believed that garlic, ginger, and turmeric had some medicinal values although there was no scientific proof. He always ate extra ginger when he drank whiskey, much like the way we have it with sushi these days, and he took one clove of garlic daily for as long as I can remember.

We often laughed when he said that, owing to his intake of garlic, he did not have any arthritic symptoms. I teased him and said I thought it was actually the beneficial effect of the whiskey that he liked.

We talked about the fact that Hindus believed the soul to be free to either merge with Brahma or be reincarnated until it was fit to dwell in eternal harmony. The pyramids were built for the Egyptian kings when they were laid to rest, thus providing a comfortable home for the body to prevent decay and also for the soul or *ka*, which continued to inhabit the body.

He always expressed great respect for older civilizations. He thought acupuncture was definitely a useful clinical tool, but he did not know anyone in the city who had learned to use its technique. Now we have learned that it is indeed valuable in pain modulation and possibly works by neuroelectric stimulation of the neuropeptides. In the past, it was believed to induce healing by removing a metaphysical *Qi* substance.

Exercise and yoga were his pet topics. He knew about the *chakras*, as described in the Tantric books as energy meridians, and he thought there may be truth in therapeutic touch in healing people.

There were excellent schools for homeopathy and ayurvedic medicines in India. He thought that in certain chronic illnesses, particularly warts, homeopathy was quite useful. He liked the idea of using the lowest possible concentration of the medicine in treating illnesses and also the principle of stimulating the healing powers of the body by reproducing some of the symptoms. This is quite different from allopathic medicine where we use much larger doses of medicine and we often treat symptoms.

He often mentioned from the Mahabharata (Indian epic mythology) and Ramayana (another epic) about Hanuman (the monkey god) who carried the mountain to find a healing plant in the Himalayas. We talked about reserpine (medicine for treating high blood pressure—rauwolfia alkaloids) and quinine (for treating malaria—cinchona) and aspirin (from willow) and other medications that are obtained from plants. More recently, we have learned that the most important medicine for treating ovarian cancer has been found in the bark of the yew tree.

He came home for lunch at one-thirty, had lunch at two and then a nap, and was on the road at four in the afternoon. He always had a very elaborate lunch of at least five or six courses served by the cook, and ate only one item at a time so he could enjoy the taste. If something was not right, he taught the cook at his next opportunity. As he would lie down for his nap, someone would massage his legs and someone else would scratch his back, all as parts of payment of some nature. It is possible that my dad had paid the dowry for the back scratcher's daughter's wedding or paid for the funeral of the masseuse's grandfather. He never discussed in the house as to who was going to be present; all were welcome, and we only found out when they were there. It was a bazaar in which the owner knew everyone. There was some sort of trade in operation almost all the time.

In the afternoon, he went to a second office where he had coffee with some of his friends, and then arrived at his dispensary in the evening. Here, the patients were informed that between seven and nine everyone was to be seen for free.

Once, my wife and I went straight to his dispensary from the airport and took a number, and he was overjoyed to have a break. He came home at ten and always had three shots of whiskey and discussed philosophy and the futility of living. He often said that life is only temporary, and we should make the best of it. He did not believe in reincarnation, but was a strong believer in predestination. He often talked to me about the fact that every action has a consequence. "Have a good today so that in the future you can have a wonderful past. When we grow old, our brain can't remember too many new things. It is our past we marvel on," he would say to me after we both had a bit to drink. He thought that even at his age, he could drink me under the table. He said, *"Khoka* (little boy), I have gained in life more than anybody can imagine." He knew the writings in the *Bhagavad Gita* and the *Bible*, and the fact that our responsibility lies in our actions and not in the results. In all the years I knew him, he never drank more than three measured shots of whiskey, and was extremely upset with my attitude of drinking to satisfaction and forgetting about measurements.

He often reminded me that level of satisfaction changes depending on the state of the mind, as we are all vulnerable to greed and indulgence. However, man should enjoy the fruits of his labor to moderation. My father knew this from the Sanskrit literature, but stated that it is written in the *Bible* as well. I later read in Ecclesiastes what my father had said many years earlier: "I know that there is no good in them but for a man to rejoice and to do good in his life. And also that every man should eat and drink and enjoy the good of all his labor, it's the gift of God" (Eccles. 3:12-14).

He had many women friends or "sisters," as he called them, who cooked for him, rubbed his head, and just made him feel good. He had given up sex since my mom's death, but had the most fulfilling life with friends and family and lived in an environment of constant entertainment.

He loved to feed people, and he entertained often more than three hundred persons during the *puja* (much like Christmas in India). He believed that good food fostered friendship and made life mellow. I guess it is much like the way women were taught in America, that the way to a man's heart is through his stomach.

I almost always gave him company by sitting next to him while he ate his light dinner. He believed in Pavlov's experiment that gastric juice is secreted when it is programmed by consistency of time. This was his personal time, and he did not like it at all if the phone rang or if he had to go to see someone during this time of the night. He went to bed at twelve-thirty, and soon it was time to go to swim.

My father never worked on Saturdays or Sundays; those days were his personal time to read, gamble, fish, and talk to family members if they came along with him. His patients were from all classes of people and with different resources. I remember an older Jewish man who loved me very much. He was a diabetic, and my father would check on him occasionally. One time, I asked him to adopt me because somehow it seemed that his life was less hectic. My father did not approve of that idea. Mr. Abraham was a charitable man, and I was the beneficiary of several gifts when he passed on after many wonderful years.

My father and I often traveled on the train to go fishing. One time, someone stole my father's wallet on the train. I was surprised the next day when this someone was apologizing to my father for having not recognized him in a crowded train in Calcutta. I learned that our chauffeur knew the leaders of most of the important thieves, that is, those who stole the most. I think he had to make a couple of phone calls to resolve the situation. We had occasional problems with theft. One night, someone not known to us was walking through the house and all the adults chased him and tried to catch him, but because the perpetrator was naked and greased, he slipped away for a while. He was eventually tackled and tied to the lamppost while everybody went back to sleep. In the morning, it was simply decided not to involve the police, and, therefore, a bucket of poison ivy was poured on his naked torso and he was allowed off the rope. I believe we were free from these types of interruptions for a long time.

My father was very resourceful and a practical man, and usually tried to avoid conflict and confrontation. I felt one time that I needed glasses, particularly as some of my friends thought I'd look cool in them. My father examined me and asked me to read a chart that I read but made many mistakes deliberately. He sent me to his eye doctor friend whom I respected. After a thorough examination, he gave me some glasses that he already had in his drawer. I wore them religiously for two months or so. Eventually, I decided that my eyes had improved enough, and I didn't need to resort to such cumbersome crutches. I was reexamined by the ophthalmologist and was told that my eyes were normal. It took me many years to understand that I was never told that my eyes were abnormal when the glasses were given. I was merely given plain glasses to satisfy my need at that time. I have learned to respect physicians' time from this lesson!

Despite incidents like this, my father was very tolerant of me. I sustained a serious fracture of my medial malleolus (inside bone near the ankle) by jumping from a second-story-high rope. I was told to slide down after I had climbed it in a regular rope-climbing class. I did not obey. I was afraid that my hands would be ruined, so I jumped. Regardless, I needed a cast, which my father placed, and I was told that it would stay on for six weeks to three months, depending on the healing process. However, my father replaced the cast several times because I accidentally lost several rulers inside it while scratching the intense itchiness caused by the sweating inside the cast. I tried with all my power to suck the foot in, much like we do to our stomach, to get those pieces of flat, wooden sticks out. Unfortunately, I couldn't gain any space to stick my finger in these cramped quarters walled by the thick plaster of paris.

· · · · ·

I grew up in a Hindu home where a strong faith in God was evident in most activities. My father performed *durga puja* (worshipped the incarnate goddess who fought evil to bring good on earth) in the house every year as long as he lived to honor his mother. He believed in all religions, and said that every religion started out with a good purpose to provide moral guidance, but the priests added their touches and introduced rituals that confused many believers.

I loved my father very much, and I saw him six months before his death. He told me that I did not need to see him at his deathbed. I did not.

· · · · ·

I loved traveling in a palanquin. I used to leave early morning with my *Da* (grandfather) to see patients. He lived about fifteen miles outside Calcutta and was the only doctor in that whole area. Fifteen miles was a lot of distance in those days, because even in a car it took about one and a half hours. The roads were less than perfect, with too many pedestrians. Four fellows carried us on their shoulders and walked with a rhythm and chanted rhythmic sounds. Grandmother gave us *chappati* (Indian bread), vegetables, and cold water in a clay pitcher. I took my slate and slate pencil for writing because Da didn't like me to use paper, as he believed that writing on paper at that age precludes sharpening the memory. I learned Sanskrit, English, mathematics, and Bengali from him. When we neared our destination, Da would ride his bicycle, which was tied to the top of the *palki* (palanquin). He then used his bicycle to go on the rice fields with his black bag while the men who brought us would entertain me. We would usually come home just before dark.

We often had some snacks and sweets, and then it was my job to light the petromax lamps and lanterns. Grandmother always helped me. We didn't have electricity in our house until I was almost eight years old, although there were electric lampposts on the streets. Grandfather taught the neighborhood children, I believe, three times a week in our courtyard. I was the only one who didn't have to do any homework.

We had dinner after everyone left. We usually sat on the floor on little mats (*aasans*) while grandmother served us several items, such as meat, fish, and two or three vegetables in little containers, and the rice or *luchi* (Bengali puffed bread made with white flour and deep fried) on the *thali* (brass plates). We always had sweets at the end.

Grandmother always ate after we finished. In those days, women fed the men first. Indian women have a total and subtle control in the family, but it is done in such a subdued and discreet manner that the men always are made to feel as though they have the power. Almost everything that happened in that house was because Grandmother wished it to happen, yet Grandfather never felt as though he were not the he-man. These men are not henpecked, but there is an understanding that depicts the women to be subdued. I guess they might have followed what Paul said to Titus (2:5), that "wives should be obedient to their own husbands." But these were, of course, written long after the Indian culture started.

After dinner, we sat on the patio or lay down and talked. We read Ramayana and Mahabharata until about nine o'clock. I recall a poem describing the need for sufficient sleep to be healthy. I always went to bed at nine and got up at five in the morning. We were relaxed in the evenings, yet vigilant and observant about any unforeseen dangers that lurked in the surroundings. I never saw any tigers in the night although I read William Blake's "Tyger, tyger, burning bright/In the forests of the night."

However, my grandparents told me a story about when they saw a tiger in our neighborhood and how it had attacked someone. I had met this man who had only one arm because a tiger ate the other. I also learned about a brave man who had killed this desperado that had developed a taste for human flesh. He told me that the South China tiger is the smallest among tigers and has the most distinctive cranial character. He knew that the Amur tiger of Siberia and northern Korea was the largest. The Royal Bengal tiger was the most magnificent of all because of its stripes and eyes.

It was not uncommon for us to see snakes at times. This particular slithery colorful rope with venomous instincts had produced a feeling in me, which is correctly described as beyond a healthy respect. I was so frightened after I had seen a child who was bitten by a snake that I absolutely refused to go to the outhouse.

We did not have indoor plumbing in those days, and Grandfather understood that even if he had stood by me, it would not alleviate my fear. We had just finished Rudyard Kipling's *Jungle Book,* and, therefore, it was decided that I should have my personal Riki Tiki Tavi (mongoose). It was kept tied with a leash next to the area of excretion. I suffered from milk allergy and amebiasis quite often, and my personal giant rat and I saw each other frequently. It provided me with a halo of freedom from fear during this most essential task of life. This act of love my grandparents demonstrated by giving me my own mongoose gave me much confidence in life. My memory for the animal made me want to present an aardvark to the Louisville Zoo, provided they would allow me to take it for a walk on a leash. Sadly, this was not possible because of some insurance problems, and thus I have remained unfulfilled in that special dream.

• • • • •

Da had never been to a movie, and I convinced him that I wanted to see a movie about Mt. Kailash (in Tibet) only with him. We got into a cycle rickshaw and arrived at the movie theater. I remember quite vividly that no more than ten minutes had passed when I had an accident and we had to come home to wash my pants. My grandfather died without ever seeing a movie!

We were up many nights because Da had to go and see sick patients. I usually did not go with him this late at night. Once, I chose to go with him after seeing the scout who came to take Da, a scene that is vivid in my mind because of its colorful nature. We went in our horse carriage in the middle of the night. I walked behind Da as he went into this courtyard, which was full of people. There were two persons with brooms standing in front of a man. The man looked disheveled and tired. His eyes were red and appeared to look ferocious. He had a ver-milion dot on his forehead, and he was standing inside a perimeter drawn by chalk on the brick floor, muttering some words in a language not commonly heard in this area. I soon realized that what he was saying didn't make any sense at all. Da talked to the leader, and the crowd was dispersed.

I learned later that this man possibly had had a seizure and post ictal confusion. A broom was used to beat him during the seizure. A piece of leather shoe or such was placed in his mouth during the carnage to drive the evil spirit away. A gag was essential to keep the mouth open, as this was the escape route for this malevolent wisp of air. I thought the convulsing maniac could have done without the markings of the broom on his body. However, the leader claimed that he alone was empowered to see the infamous apparition when it would bugger off the oral orifice. This rather less than welcoming greeting was essential for its extraction. It is only by this technique that the demon would be released in a subdued manner without causing any further harm whenever it occupied such a diminutive human body. He was a small person who looked extremely emaciated. I was told that these kinds of spirits enter the bodies only when the body becomes excessively weak. At this time, I did not know much about exorcism that was practiced elsewhere.

I asked Da to be sure and not let me be a weak body. There were many nights when I could not fall asleep after being involved in such exciting events, but on such special days I slept late because I never had to go to school. I remember asking Da if I could be the leader one time, and often he would take too long to answer me and I would fall asleep by then. I told him once that he probably did not have the power to make me a leader anyway. He told me a story about a little boy who went to the mountain with his father when his father had claimed that he could make the world dark but that it would involve very hard work. So, they were sitting and the eclipse came and the world was dark. Soon enough, it was light again. The little boy was excited. He clapped. He begged his dad to do it again.

Dad said he was too tired now. It would take him a long time to perform an encore.

· · · · ·

We always had some fluid before going to bed. It was determined that I should have goat's milk. However, Da always had a glass of milk and a black pill that grandmother served him. I always thought that there was something special about this pill because it was kept under lock and key. Every Saturday we used to go with a ration card to a government shop where Da would get exactly one week's supply of this pill. I could never convince Da to trade my special milk for his special pill. These pills were served in a package of broad leaves much enjoyed by goats, and there was always a group of docile goats of unknown owners that frequented the perimeter of this shop where the customers discarded the leaves after they had taken the last pill.

One time, I went there, only to learn that the shop had been relocated at a different site for about a week. I was amazed at the aggressiveness of these goats that butted me and almost knocked me down. They appeared rather disturbed and had lost their look of limpid bedroom eyes. I later learned that these goats were just as much addicted to this product of poppy seeds as the people were, except the goats got the leaves for free. I did not believe the financial issues were as important to the goats. I believe the deprivation and the sudden withdrawal that had occurred without notice had created a herd of tremulous, agitated goats. Many cows of unknown owners would also hang around this addict zone, very much like anywhere else in India. I was glad that I was not attacked by an opium-addicted cow suffering from drug withdrawal. The newspapers would have said, "Young boy aggravated holy cow and pierced himself while assaulting a peaceful animal." The normal fine of two hundred rupees for hitting a cow would possibly have been excused owing to my grandfather's status in the community.

I remember those evenings of doldrums when we sat outside in the field in front of our house. I carried a hand fan to move the air and cool off from the humidity that would make us sweat just for existing. Sometimes a little breeze would pick up and a few thin, white sheets of clouds would float through the blue sky. Da liked to recite Kalidas's *MeghDoot* (the Sanskrit writing about the cloud messenger). He told me about the clouds that carried messages to distant lands to their lovers. He thought some of them changed their shapes and surprised their mates, and others lacked the persistence and the commitment necessary to have a relationship and, therefore, became rain. We discussed the different shapes and how they entangled and embraced their yakshi mates who were patiently waiting for their friendly wind to give a boost to hasten the arrival of their consort. He said the reflections of the sun's rays made a shining crown on all the clouds that were falling behind and made them appear more attractive for the impatient lover. I didn't like the clouds before the rain because they were always in a hurry. I have always liked a slower pace in affairs of love. Da was a rather quiet sort of a person, and he told me that real excitement in life is attained only with a patient listening to one's feelings.

In the late evenings we would talk, but often would be interrupted by the loudness of the gossipy frogs. I guess they told each other about the bugs they ate and the fish they saw or just what it was like in a regular frog day.

I asked him how he found Grandmother. He told me their parents arranged the marriage when she was only three years old, and she came to be with him when she became fourteen after "she had some sort of changes" in her body, as he put it. This is when the actual marriage took place. I fully understood the meaning of what he said only when my body changed as well. He said he learned to love her, and she learned to be a doctor's wife and accepted life as it was given to her. He thought she was wonderful, and the feeling was mutual. They had a tremendous respect for each other.

He said he loved me the same way as that and explained that I was given to him. He did not know me before I arrived on my mom's lap. It was his duty and responsibility to love me, he explained, and then this special feeling for me would well up to him, as we would get to know each other. He was pleased the way he felt about me. I told him that I was going to find my own bride, and he held me and wept that he would not be here to see the choices I made. He knew I would be honorable, and that he would be satisfied with my choices. He really trusted in me, which made me feel really happy.

I asked him how he chose my father for his daughter. He told me that when my father was twenty-one, my grand-mother saw him playing volleyball in our field. My grandmother had Da make the contact with my dad's family, and thus my mom was betrothed. This is the way things happened in those days in respectable families who were well placed in life.

I remember attending many weddings. The family and the relatives of the groom came to the bride's house where the actual ceremony took place. All the women were dressed in beautiful and colorful *saris* and the men wore *dhoti* (a white cloth rapped around the waist hanging up to the ankle in an organized, pleated fashion). All the ceremony usually took place in a courtyard or hallway, where the father of the bride bequeathed the daughter in front of a fire built of sandalwood. Fire (*agni*) is considered the ultimate witness, because it can burn and cleanse. Then, the priests read parts of the holy books and then knots were tied in a symbolic manner on the clothes connecting the bride and the groom. The groom and the bride exchanged *lehs* (garlands made of flowers). Guests brought gifts, and there was always a lot of small talk and niceties exchanged and a big feast followed. I always enjoyed this part. In some families, the bride's father gave a dowry to the husband and in reality to the new family so that they could start a life together.

I fell in love with the most beautiful girl in Louisville, who was a student nurse, and subsequently a courtship led to our wedding. She had honored me by asking me to discuss a paper she had presented in one of her conferences. I recall discussing with my father-in-law after couple of years about a dowry he might have owed me! I believe he bought us our first grill, which we enjoyed for many years.

· · · · ·

My father's family was very active in the non-cooperation movement of Mahatma Gandhi, and my uncle (my father's older brother) was an important member of the Gandhi movement. My prospective maternal relatives were very prominent in the society as well. Thus the marriage of my parents was sealed by reputation. I believe I had seen a commercial about Rolls Royce once when a fellow went for a test drive and was concerned that the car didn't have any gas. However, the dealership informed him that he should not worry because Rolls Royce does not need gas, that it runs on reputation. My father took a year off from college to participate in the non-cooperation movement, during which time he did not wear any clothes made by British looms in the factories.

There was very strong anti-British sentiment in our house. They had just been driven out after exploiting us for years. It was always taken for granted in our home that we were just fine and did not need approval from someone else to be content. I was always told that if I ever went to school, I should not worry about the grades, because I was already an "A," and, therefore, all I had to do was to do my part with love and caring. This is one of the main teachings of the *Bhagavad Gita*—that our responsibility lies in our action and not in the result. This, incidentally, has a close association and a flavor of predestination, as the Presbyterians believe. However, in many other aspects of life, I was told just to have fun and I did not have to do my best. I liked that very much. This made me feel that I could ride a bicycle without having to compete or swim without having to worry that I was not swimming fast enough. I could goof around if that's what I chose to do. It was fun, and there was no pressure.

$$\bullet \ \bullet \ \bullet \ \bullet \ \bullet$$

I read the headlines of the newspaper every morning to Da. He, in turn, helped me with the pronunciation and explained the words to me. We spoke in Bengali at home. I read Aesop's *Fables* and learned about persistence—try and try again until you succeed at last. I learned about resilience and about my happiness not causing anyone else any sadness, such as the story of throwing rocks in a well to watch the ripples but all the while endangering the lives of the frogs that live in it.

It was a simple life as a child in India. We brushed our teeth with twigs of a neem tree. Sometimes we used the ash from the stove that was still left over from cooking the previous night. We used well water that was purified by throwing potassium permanganate in it. We bathed in the water from the well or a tubule, which I enjoyed very much. I remember that I had to put the whole weight of my body to lower the handle far enough to get any water out of it. I was often told not to play with it, but I liked it because it gave me resistance, I think. I learned soon enough that the resistance was not without danger. One day, I slipped, sustaining a significant cut under my chin from this metallic unfriendly swing of mine, which left a scar that reminds me still of my disobedience.

During this time, I had a slingshot and knocked down papayas with it. The servant picked the good ones by climbing a ladder so the fruits wouldn't be bruised. My grandmother never ate any chicken eggs because she believed the chicken to be a Muslim, and, therefore, only duck eggs were used in the main kitchen. We ate chicken eggs in a separate place, away from the main cooking area. I noticed that the people who cleaned the toilet or such—that is, the outhouse—had to announce themselves because grandmother had to take a bath, in case she stepped in their shadow. One time I asked her what she would do if by chance she saw them while they were cleaning the toilet. She told me not to ask such ridiculous questions. It was incredible to see such dichotomy in the relationship with people. Da held the people close when they touched his feet in reverence. He talked to them with respect, and quite often did not take any money for his services if he thought that they did not have enough to eat. But Da always changed his shirt before he sat down to eat.

He saw patients in his dispensary, which was across from the courtyard in front of the house. Every morning, there was a gathering of a large number of people outside the house, waiting to be seen for some ailment or other. Many coughed, smoked *bidi* (a local Indian cigarette made by rolling tobacco leaves), and spat on the ground. We had a beautiful yard bordering the courtyard, with red and yellow hibiscus, some roses, and marigolds and yellow flowers that had some medicinal properties as far as I was concerned. I often injured myself, as most children do. The neighbor children who played with me told me to rub the leaves of marigold and this other flower to my wounds, which always grew in a rather prolific manner next to the outhouse. This always stopped the bleeding.

The barn was one floor and was located just beyond the yard. The woman who cleaned our house lived on one side. Adjacent to her room, we had a cow and the horse. The horse carriage was kept on the opposite side of the barn. She collected cow dung and made it into round patties that she dried on the back wall and used as her cooking fuel. There was a field next to it on which we often lay. Here we rested and read at times. The pond was located next to the field on the side. There was a railroad track right across all this. I often watched the train. This was my entertainment. There was not much else to do in this town those days.

Da said that the fish in the water grew bigger and faster owing to the noise of the train. They constantly ran and got a lot of exercise that way. I believe there were some poppy plants that grew wild next to the pond. They grew only for the pleasure of growing, just like the rest of us in the neighborhood. No one smoked pot where I grew up. My father offered me *bhang* (soup of the paste from the bark of the marijuana plant) when I was about twelve. I slept many hours after that. I never had a desire to taste it again.

• • • • •

There was love and a bond between the children, but

within this group somehow I felt I did not belong. I felt emptiness whenever I was playing, and there was restlessness within me. I did not know the reason for it at that time. I just did not feel fulfilled. I did not know the meaning of the word at that time, of course. I was like a caged bird that wanted to get out although I had everything imaginable in the cage. Somehow someone else's yard looked prettier. Perhaps, at that time I did not know about thistles. I felt that the time of confinement and conception was over, and I was ready for the contractions to push me out. I realized at an early age that what I would see at first during the passage might make me cry. But I needed that strong breath that would make me cry because constant happiness was smothering me. I did not realize how quickly the inevitable would happen.

The umbilical cord was cut. Da died when I was ten. There was no tombstone that said, "And curst be he who moves my bones." Da was cremated.

The next day, many people came to our house to pay respect to a man who had truly loved them. Almost everybody in and around the town was his patient. He had delivered most of the younger people, although they were much older than I was. Many of them sobbed and some consoled me, as I wept nonstop. Although my uncle was a doctor in the town, already everybody still considered me as truly one of their own. They expected me to become a doctor and return to this town to practice. I was Da's shadow, and everyone knew that.

He lay on a bed, and the body was covered with a new, white cloth that was completely blanketed by the flowers given by almost everyone who came to see him. He was a grandfather to many, friend to most, and Daaktarbabu (doctor) to everyone. People assigned by my uncle carried him on their shoulders to the *ghat*, where he was placed on a pyre of sandalwood. My Da was gone forever to the clouds. I could not touch him any-more. I continued to believe that he was watching me. Some-times, when nobody was looking, I would talk to him. I shared my thoughts with him for many years. He is living with me even now. The warmth of his touch encourages me. I weep at times because I can't touch him, and I still wish that my head could be next to his pillow.

· · · · ·

My friends and I used to go watch people when they were being cremated. Actually, we used to go to the place next to the river where bricks were made. All the cremation was carried out close to the river. I did not have a child's bike, so I used to ride Da's bike. My legs would be going like scissors. We carried a small bag of potatoes, and a little salt and pepper with us. We would stick the potatoes in the ground and place a small marker on this underground kiln. When the stick was all burnt up, we would know that the potatoes were baked as well. We would eat the potatoes and watch the smoke of someone being cremated at a distance. We never heard anyone crying or wailing. There was a silence through which one could hear the song of the river, a quiet song. The river had to run. It could not stop. Of course, it didn't know where it was going and didn't know the dangers on the way. Wherever it would end, was that the designated place?

I wondered if it had known what Ralph Waldo Emerson had said in "Brahma":

Far or forgot to me is near;
Shadow and sunlight are the same;
The vanished gods to me appear;

And one to me are shame and fame.

The song was interrupted by the intruding voice of the paddles of a boat or two. People were going home after the day's work was done. The flame would rise against the background of the night sky to consume the darkness. It made scary shadows, like tongues of dragons and feet of alligators. At least, that is what we thought then. It seemed to flaunt its arrogance for a minute or two. Soon, it was consumed by the darkness. Fire ran out of wood. We never talked about it because it did not mean very much to us. Sometimes we would buy a stick of sugarcane and chew it while we walked back. Later on, if someone asked us how far we had walked, we would say "about three feet of sugarcane." Those days of growing up were truly wonderful. We never dreamed we would be grownups.

I felt angry that my Da was gone. I did not go to the ghat to see his cremation. As a matter of fact, I didn't understand exactly what happened. He and I used to sleep inside the same mosquito net in the beginning of every night, although I used to wake up on another bed. My grandmother was always next to him in the morning. He explained to me that he was not sure how this exactly happened, but he wanted me to check on it.

Anyway, he used to pray every night. I always lay next to him. One warm March night, he fell down on the bed while sitting and praying. When I called Grandmother, he never spoke to anyone. God and I were the two persons he spoke to last. He was the most wonderful grandfather! I cried for three months when he died.

Sometimes my grandpa and I would sit next to the pond and throw in a line. There would always be a fish at the end of the line, but we would let it go. I mostly enjoyed throwing a flat rock or a piece of a clay pot into the pond in a manner that it would hop and dive and then skim on the water. We would both try to see who could make his stone jump the most times. At times, we just watched the ripples in the water. There would often be water hyacinth at one or the other corner of the pond. I loved to see the frogs jump from one leaf to the other. All the tadpoles would scurry along to bed in a chaotic manner at the sound of this knock. I guess we often interrupted the sibling bonding experience. I sometimes held a frog in my hand, then it just jumped off when I opened my palm.

I remember Da would tell me not to be a "big mango" in life because it loses its taste and aroma. He would say be a *kohitoor* (a very expensive small and sweet mango that grows only in a special part of Bengal). He said that an uneducated man often has pomp like a soda water bottle, and, once the fizz goes, no one has any use for the bottle. He liked people with substance and without vanity. He taught me to be happy with ninety-nine rupees and not try to make it one hundred by making everyone unhappy in the process. He talked in many different ways to explain to me about desires in life. He knew a lot about contentment and greed.

I had a personal barber who always came to the house on a certain day and cut my hair while I sat on a chair wearing a cloak made of newspaper. He charged only twenty cents. I once went to the local barbershop and had a haircut, and I believe he charged my grandfather almost a dollar, which caused a bit of unhappiness. After my marriage, my wife found this interesting, and she cut my hair for many years to give me this special joy of having my hair cut at home.

Da would ask me to recite "The Daffodils" and "Solitary Reaper," and often asked me questions from *Maxim Gorky* or *Treasure Island*. When my children were younger, I asked them to memorize poems of Ogden Nash. The poems were a little different, like "The Turtle":

> The turtle lives 'twixt plated decks
> Which practically conceal its sex.
> I think it clever of the turtle
> In such a fix to be so fertile.

Now, when we have a recitation, we all laugh because we choose funny poems. I often share the tender memories I had with my grandfather when he was alive. Those were very special moments, because we were just friends—I was just younger than he, that's all!

One afternoon, I was rather frightened to see him in his dispensary with a snake around his neck. A man was standing in front of him telling him something. I turned around. I ran to tell Grandmother, but the man removed the snake as soon as Da agreed to visit his wife. Da left that instant and followed him on his bicycle to the home of the snake charmer. I always felt that the snake charmer should have used a different form of inducement for the doctor. On many such visits, there was no monetary exchange, but what was exchanged could never have been bought with money—all these people truly loved my grandfather. They respected him for just being there.

Almost everyone owed my grandfather. The harvest party was the occasion when all the debts were settled. The annual party after the harvest was a memorable occasion. People came in bullock carts and bicycles. Many came by foot. Some of them brought us a goat or rice and vegetables, some brought handmade mats. We used the smaller ones for sitting and the larger ones for lying. Most people stayed for a day in our field. They had a good meal in our house, and the New Year started. No one owed anybody anything except goodwill and brotherhood after this. Thus did life go on around these simple folks.

I believe Gray describes it the best in "Elegy Written in a Country Churchyard":

Let not ambition mock their useful toil
Their homely joys, and destiny obscure.

I told Da one day that I would go away to a distant land. I wanted to see what the clouds looked like in another country. I just wanted to have fun all the time. He always listened. I remember when I was about nine years old telling him that I was going to be a brain surgeon. He hugged me and wept. I knew what that meant. I was afraid of that, too. He told me later that he would be watching me, no matter where I would be. He would be in the sky, and he would be able to see far away from there.

His frugal behavior helped me to understand the value of saving money for the days ahead. He always said not to light a candle in the daytime, because then in the evening we would not have any light. I started saving as soon as my children were born so that I could be financially independent. Moreover, that way I could retire from this type of practice to a different kind if I so desired. I learned to invest wisely. I knew that in a capitalist world, financial freedom was mandatory to be able to pursue other interests. I knew that money could be made through investments. I bought Chrysler stock in the early eighties when all of my friends were buying boats. Everybody thought that Chrysler would go bankrupt. I wrote to Mr. Iacocca about designing a convertible. His chief engineer wrote me back that it was already in the process.

I enjoyed the boats when I got invited without the hassle of the upkeep. My stock appreciated. I discovered another important reason to become financially independent, particularly for a specialist like myself. It became apparent to me that general practitioners had considerable control over my referral pattern. I would have to invite them to dinner or play golf with them or just participate in gratuitous gestures only because they referred me patients. Most of the time there was a subtle controlling effect. I was delighted when I was able to cut this bond and regain my freedom. I enjoyed my practice more. My practice expanded, despite those who were rather envious of my individuality and independence. I noticed that when I became independent, very few invited me to anything. It is only then that I realized the difference between friendship and a business relationship, which in my naiveté had escaped me.

• • • • •

I often smoked the butts of the bidis thrown on the grass, which were still lighted. I had a difficult time finding matches in the daytime, because Grandmother did not approve of playing with fire. Da told me that I could get tuberculosis by smoking leftover bidis from the patients, but I was not about to pay heed to such big words used as a scare tactic. However, one day I saw him take a big needle attached to a pipe from a bottle kept inside a large box and stick it in a person's chest. I heard the patient moan painfully. This really scared me. He explained that the person has tuberculosis, and he is giving the diseased lung some rest. I never smoked any leftover bidi after watching that episode. I have always been scared of needles. I asked my companions about it, and they were not fond of needles either. I learned later that the procedure was called AP or artificial pneumothorax. That was the accepted treatment of the day to collapse the diseased lung while it was healing. I had asked him if he knew for sure which one to collapse. He told me that sometimes he didn't know if both lungs were equally affected or not.

I was home schooled, and Da was my teacher. He taught me through lessons and by assigning me several responsibilities. He showed me how to check if the needles were sharp by scratching them upside down on a slate. He filed them down, and Grandmother boiled the syringes and needles so that he could use them over. Most of the patients didn't have a spoon. My job was to cut paper in a zigzag fashion that would match approximately a spoon size and paste it in front of the bottles. Grandmother usually boiled the bottles to sterilize them. The compounder then dispensed the red or green mixture and placed a new cork on top of each of the bottles. I was always fascinated by the color changes. I believe my childhood fascination led me to get a certification as a mixologist after I became a neurosurgeon. I had learned to make castor oil emulsion, which took a lot of patience. I had learned Tinc. Rhei. Co. (a common medicine prescribed for indigestion)—cardamom, caraway, cochineal, cinnamon, glycerin, and alcohol. A common laxative prescribed in those days consisted of senna, sucrose, fennel fruit, and sublime sulfur with licorice root. I watched him set fractures and place splints. He sometimes reduced shoulder dislocations as well.

In the evenings, we would sit in the living room or lie on a bed and talk about Mt. Kailash, Mansarowar, and many other places Grandfather wanted to go. He was unable to fulfill his dreams of traveling. He told me about Timor the Lane, Attila the Hun, and the Khyber Pass. I would be ready and excited to see these places. I visited my memory land quite often, particularly whenever I was by myself. I told him that I would ask God to fill his cup through my activities. I told him that every place that I would visit, I would quietly say a prayer for him. He loved the idea. He thought I should climb the mountains slowly, because he had read that some people get headaches and die when they are in a hurry. He had read that between 37-32 B.C., Too-Kin, a high Chinese official, had reported on the difficulties of the soldiers crossing Kilik Pass into Afganisthan. It was called the Great Headache Mountain. Now, of course, we have identified the condition better, and we call it acute mountain sickness. The first high-altitude laboratory was set up on Mont Blanc sometime in 1787. We are beginning to learn about the possible role of increased brain water in the production of high altitude pulmonary edema and the difficulties associated with it.

I talked with Da about my new bamboo fishing pole. I had learned to cover up some dirt with plastic and then discover a lot of worms underneath it. Even though I didn't like the slimy feeling of worms, I didn't mind hooking them to the hook anymore. I talked about how I had discovered a patch on the grass turning yellow where a brick covered it. I had also learned to gig a frog at the neighbor's pond. Da taught me that it is the chlorophyll in the plants that imparts the green color. He told me that in some countries before winter, the leaves change color from lack of moisture and that the chlorophyll undergoes degeneration. I talked a lot while grandpa listened. Sometimes he also answered. But I would hear him snoring at times. His pillow was higher than mine was, and so I could not see his eyes. There were times when I would have to repeat everything because I thought he hadn't heard me the first time. I thought he was too proud to admit that he fell asleep. The monotonous noise of the crickets would finally lull me to sleep. I would be lying down watching the geckos on the wall catching the flying insects. I could hear Grandmother's fading annoyed voice at

Grandfather for keeping me up so late. I would dream of giant alligators walking on a desert. The alligators would then eat up the people sitting next to an oasis while they were taking a break from the sun. I would suddenly wake up from my sleep, crying. Grandmother would hold me and scratch my back. Sometimes, I wasn't sure if I had a dream of alligators or if I had faked it for the attention. It felt good regardless of the intention, but I always thought that possibly it was more fun if the intent was deceitful.

One of the reasons I liked my father then was because I could just relax, but with Da I kind of felt as though I had to do the right thing all the time. I remember once that it was decided that I needed a spanking. Grandmother summoned my uncle. He took me to his room and then told me behind closed doors that because I was the son of his sister who had died, he could not spank me, but it would be OK to act in front of Grandma as though I were in pain. However, I was told not to lie if I was asked directly. I was never asked. I often took advantage of this kind-ness for my personal benefit.

I worked in my garden and grew eggplants and pumpkins and okras. Da gave me a spot in the main garden that was all for me, and I could do whatever I wanted with it. I chose to use it to grow vegetables and some flowers, such as zinnias and cosmos. I liked the colors, and I learned that the flowers would distract the bugs. I often had good luck. We ate a lot of vegetables owing to my success of growing an abundance of greens.

Later on in life, I learned to fry the pumpkin flowers, and often served them as a delicious appetizer to go with a glass of wine. Moreover, I knew that I only needed one pumpkin flower to grow a big one! My vegetable growing spirit has remained with me. Just a few years ago, I grew a one hundred and twenty-pound pumpkin, which would have won the pretty pumpkin award at the state fair. I didn't take it to the state fair, but I took many pictures. I started it on a plastic sheet, and then placed a couple of two-by-fours underneath it so my son and I could lift it. I love growing irises now. I have organized my iris patch as soldiers and as books in the libraries. I often sit next to my iris library and study them. However, my iris soldiers are wearing purple and red berets and sway with the wind in unison, all the while saluting with their fluffed petals. The baby sheep butt at these aggressive enemies whose resilience springs them back to stand their ground. The little lamb feels sheepish at its inability to defeat such a colorful enemy. It walks away to its ignominy without having tarnished its innocence or its youthful vigor. I watch the little lamb sit down to ponder with a small blade of grass in its mouth. I determine from the somber look on its face that it is planning the next move. It is free and frivolous. It is frisky, and just jumps around as though it has discovered new freedom. Sometimes it just rubs against its sibling. Then both of them take a nap to replenish their energy expended during such a joyous exercise.

I raise animals, vegetables, and flowers on my farm. I have many goats, sheep, chickens, donkeys, horses, and llamas. I learned to shear my sheep after visiting a farm in New Zealand, but I never became very adept and was always scared of those vibrating blades that didn't have any guards. I often made nicks on these poor animals, and they often ended up looking like little lions, because I gave up trying to trim wool from the neck and groin areas. Sometimes this leonine look accompanied by red stripes of scarlet made them look like sheep hippies. I painted their bodies with scarlet red at times to avoid potential infection after performing accidental shearing surgery. Despite my surgical training, they often had bleeding skin instead of just having their blanket lifted in summer. I gave up this stressful procedure for the sheep and resorted to cutting their wool with scissors. My girl and I often spent hours on an individual sheep. She subsequently gathered the wool, washed it in rainwater, and then dried it prior to carding it for spinning. The donkeys always attacked the sheep after they were sheared, mistaking them for dogs. The donkeys and dogs have permanent animosity. I admire the baby goats and the lambs. At times, several deer come to play with the animals, attracted by the salt lick in the barn.

I recall that one day after our morning reading or such when I was about five or six years old, my father took me to his house where I played with the dog. I just acted mean for some reason. I threw a hard cricket ball at the dog for it to catch instead of the rubber ball. It cried a little after jumping for it. I didn't seem to feel bad about it until ten years later. I often didn't know why I acted in such a cruel manner sometimes. My psychiatrist told me that I had an emotional deprivation syndrome—I hated him for giving it a name. I wish I could have done something so that I wouldn't have had such subconscious outbursts of anger from repressed hostility. Now, I often weep thinking how I must have hurt so many persons who tolerated me and loved me in spite of my abrasive and insensitive behavior.

My father made some futile attempts to send me to a local school after Grandfather's death, but I was not suited to the environment. I often spoke less than the truth. I gambled. I bummed cigarettes and participated in self-abuse. My schooling began when I was twelve in a school about a thousand miles away from home. I thought I had learned to be self-sufficient, but I realized later that I was quite dependent on my wife. I never understood if that was because I didn't know how to take care of myself, or if it meant I was co-dependent. I didn't understand if it was a convenient way to escape from household responsibilities. However, it became clear to me after the divorce that the dependency had added a sense of security in my love for my spouse although she might not have appreciated it. Well, now I am on my own and I am self-sufficient for sure. I am not lost anymore. The need for dependency has gone away, but I must admit there is still a vacuum that has not yet been filled. I wonder how the puppies feel when they are taken away from their mothers. Our dog seemed happy. It played. It slept and ate, but did the dog miss its mommy? I bet it did. If only we could have understood. I have talked with many people who have their mother. They don't see their mother as often as once a year, but it is like having money in the bank—you may never need it, but you just don't feel poor anymore. It is not about confidence, but it is like an extra electric blanket on a winter night. It is like having an oversized T-shirt available to us, which protects us from an unexpected chill. My T-shirt was torn twice, you see! After the divorce, I felt the blanket was gone, too. But I have successfully developed an extra shell around my cocoon so that cold air can't get in anymore. I certainly hope some gentle, warm breeze can still touch me at times. In "Shesher Kabita," Rabindranath Tagore wrote,

> Blow gently over my garden, wind of the southern sea
> When my lover cometh and calleth me.

Some evenings I was surprised by the visit of many *hijras* (men who were born with incomplete male genitalia and then had the visible parts removed by rather poorly trained surgeons. These were men who wore female clothes). These people were social outcasts and lived in areas that were not even known to me. They came whenever a newborn baby arrived in someone's home to announce it with a joyous celebration by beating on a mat with sticks. Da said he didn't know how this custom started. Pocket change and sweetened balls of rice were thrown at them. They left after that. They were never seen in the daytime because it was considered to be an ill omen for anyone else to be visible next to them. I never learned much about them until I was more than eighteen years old. Our chauffeur explained to me the gory details of the procedure that is performed to create such an outcast. This was dictated by the attitude of the people in the society who did not accept them. There was no compassion and no love for them. However, many men of society went to the red-light district, away from their wives, for a glorious night with these "freaks of nature," as they were called by the so-called reputable men in the daytime. I was glad I was born with a unisex character. I often wondered if I would have committed suicide if I had been born with such a disfigurement in a society where a birth defect was considered as though a punishment from God. This really bothered me, but I didn't know what to say, and I was never encouraged to discuss this topic—it just never came up.

However, many people believed in reincarnation in a way that I didn't quite comprehend. As a matter of fact, I guess I didn't understand God making men suffer to serve Him. He certainly knew the choices people were going to make. Surely, if it is a choice that is going to make me fall out of a window in a moving train, my heavenly Father would advise me against it. It scared me to think otherwise. I wrestled with the fear imparted on the paralyzed man who was healed by Jesus. "Behold, thou are made whole; sin no more, lest a worse thing come unto thee" (John 5:14).

I wanted a God who would love me no matter what and would protect me when I was in trouble. I didn't want a God who was always busy doing something—I wanted a God who was relaxed, and, at the same time, would look after me. I didn't want my God just to be playing with women or such while lying on a lotus. I didn't know if I was supposed to find my God, or if God the creator would stick with me. I didn't want His care of me to be transferred to a junior, such as an assistant who is in training for a higher post. As a matter of fact, I didn't understand all the incarnations that were helping us through all of our daily activities, for example, business (*ganesh*), studies (*saraswati*), wealth (*lakshmi*), and so on. It was after many years that I had the time to read the translations of the *Upanishads* and the *Bhagavad Gita* to understand the concepts. I concluded that this is not a religion for poor people, nor is this a religion for the uneducated. Particularly this religion did not serve well in a country where an overabundance of people suffered from a paucity of wealth as well as of education.

I realized God loves me and blessed me, but the Hindu God has too many employees. I think that most people don't know the real CEO of this operation. This religion is for the fortunate and the philosophers. This religion is not for everyone, because very few attain the Brahma. The path is too liberal. Too much self-study is involved to find the many ways to the truth. I had already read Malinowski's *Magic, Science and Religion*. I had read Sartre's *The Transcendence of the Ego*. My education only propelled me toward finding a God of love who would seek me out as though I was His child. I wanted to come home. I didn't know its location. I was growing. I didn't want to bend in the wind. I needed a stake. It wasn't because I was weak. It was because I wanted a friend by my side and a prescribed method of salvation—I wasn't ready for a free studying group. "I am the resurrection and the life . . . . And whosoever liveth and believeth in me shall never die" (John

11:25-26). That was good enough for me. I wanted a religion with compassion and forgiveness. I wanted to know how much God did for us after He created us. I found a God who gave his own son for us! And he does not even have a real name. He is just happy being a generic God. There is no radar that can detect Him. He has no shape or form. He is just a spirit that can whisper to me without punishing me in public. I was locked in the target for the missile to hit me from this special AWAC—I was hit—God took me in. I knew I was in the in crowd.

I accepted Christ in my life in the fall of 1979, in front of a large congregation. I was the Saul that wanted to be Paul. I wanted to believe that grace is a gift, and I didn't have to earn it. I liked the thought that if I was born blind, it was only because "the work of God will be manifested in me." I felt excited about "washing in the pool of Siloam" so I could see. I was happy to know that "I am the good shepherd, and know my sheep, and am known of mine" (John 10: 14). I didn't care to argue with thirty-nine verses as to how the miracle happened. I just became a believer. That's all there is to it! I didn't care about the Pharisees' argument about Sabbath. I am a doctor. I had to operate on any day when there was an emergency. I wanted to follow Jesus. I realized that nothing has been as fulfilling to me as the feeling I get while I sing, "My faith looks up to thee, Thou lamb of Calvary." I pray Lord cleanse the depths within my soul and the crevasses in my heart, and let resentment cease. Let old bitterness depart and make me into an instrument of yours that will sound the most harmonious when it is time to play to serve you. This, Lord, is my mission.

I believe in the resurrection of the dead. "When the dead shall hear the voice of the Son of God and they that hear shall live" (John 5:25). I really do not believe in the rein-carnation. I certainly do not believe in God doling out punishments for our sins in the form of disability or birth defects. Jesus categorically said "neither" to the blind man when He was asked if the man was blind for his sin or his father's.

I remember seeing many beggars who were disfigured by leprosy. My family did not participate in their care or in explaining to me that maybe I should learn about the condition. At that young age, I didn't understand the seriousness of the problem. My need for involvement in such a difficult area was never emphasized. Now, it is too late to do anything as a neurosurgeon. However, I visited Miraj, India, where the local doctors run a large leprosy hospital. They are working on a trial of multidrug treatment, and different plastic surgeons perform corrective surgery on deformities caused by the illness. Dapsone, solapsone, and rifampin were not available when I was young. There was a considerable lack of understanding about its different manifestations. Now, I have read just about everything Dr. P. Brandt has written on the subject. He was a young British doctor who came to India for a two-year assignment soon after World War II. He stayed for twenty-five years, adding much to the understanding of how to care for patients afflicted with leprosy. He retired in America as professor emeritus at the University of Washington at Seattle. I believe his book, *The Blessing of Pain,* should be read by everyone.

Dr. Brandt told us neurosurgeons a story once about simple ways to solve problems. In the early fifties, he noticed that some of the leprosy patients lost their implanted fingers soon after the surgery, whereas his other patients healed appropriately. He found out that rats ate the fingers of these poor, unfortunate patients who did not feel pain. He started a cat colony on the campus of the hospital and gave a kitten to every leprosy patient when they went home. The problem disappeared!

When I was a child, my father showed me a person with a thickened nerve in the neck (I now know it is the great auricular nerve). I saw him take a scraping from the nose of the patient. Later, he told me that the diagnosis of leprosy was confirmed. Leprosy is often referred to as Hansen's disease to avoid the stigma attached to the former name.

• • • • •

I went to medical school in Calcutta in 1961, where I learned medicine from some of the finest clinicians. I was lucky. I did well in anatomy, physiology, and biochemistry. I earned the dubious honor of being the senior prosector. I carried out many dissections in the night by myself. Sitting alone in the anatomy laboratory at night scared me at times. There would be about thirty dead bodies, and, obviously, no one was supposed to move except me. The slightest noise would almost always cause a panic attack in me, although I didn't believe in ghosts or such. My sister had told me once when we were both younger that ghosts don't have shadows. Somehow that thought scares me now.

I was rather sensitive to the formaldehyde that is commonly used for preserving the human parts from decaying early. One day, I passed out during the anatomy class. I awoke soon enough to find myself lying next to a dissected person. My colleagues had placed me on the nearest table to which I had fallen.

Our wards were true clinical laboratories. In one day on one side of the ward, we could see patients afflicted with cancer of the breast, cancer of the colon, and lymphoma. On the opposite side, we could see others with the diagnosis of malaria, dengue fever, or possibly someone with a tubercular pleurisy. We didn't have adequate facilities to confirm many of the diagnoses. Therefore, good clinical acumen was mandatory.

At times during the student years, we had to work in the emergency rooms to see acute problems and observe the management from senior residents. A man arrived in severe discomfort because he couldn't urinate. I was asked to catheterize him. It was at that time that I learned about the coudet (firm-tipped) catheter. A stricture possibly from past gonorrhea prevented me from passing a regular catheter. I remembered observing Da when he had treated a person possibly with a similar problem (he did not tell me the diagnosis then, as I recall). He used the stem of a papaya branch with some lubricant to accomplish the task. I still remember the patient's agonizing yelling, but he thanked Da after he was able to urinate. Many years later, I saw a man in Columbus, Ohio, who kept a catheter inside the sleeve of his hat. Whenever he had trouble, he catheterized himself using his spit!

There were no training facilities for neurological surgery at that time in Calcutta. I had made up my mind that I was going to the United States to get the necessary training and possibly return to set up a practice, if a suitable opportunity were to be found.

We were trained adequately in the diagnosis of common illnesses and their management. We still saw patients afflicted with syphilis with its protean manifestations, though much less since the availability of penicillin. We took a rotation in the infectious disease hospital to learn about the common infectious diseases, such as tetanus. I had personal experience with this particular illness. My cousin had died at the age of thirty-eight in the postoperative period after a perfectly fine hysterectomy because she had developed postoperative tetanus. At that time, it was a virtual death sentence. We didn't have a respirator, and, therefore, we took turns with the Ambu bag to ventilate her for three days after which she died from pneumonia, as she was unable to cough or breathe on her own.

We learned about filariasis in the hospital and learned to operate on hydroceles. I myself was afflicted with tropical eosinophilia (a form of filariasis caused by mosquito bites, which made my lungs look mottled on the chest X-ray. I coughed incessantly). I was treated with pentavalent antimony before hetrazan became available. I am fortunate that I do not have optic atrophy (paling of the optic disks and blindness). I am extremely glad that I did not develop hydroceles, because at a young age it is better to die of anything else besides coming to the hospital with an enlarged scrotum.

As we learned about kidney diseases, I remembered being treated for orthostatic proteinuria (passing proteins in the urine). My urine otherwise checked out all right. There was no blood or white cells. I remember my father drawing me a picture of a white-cell cast. There was no treatment available. My father told me to exercise and improve my posture so that my kidneys would not be touching my backbones or such. I believe my kidneys still touch my backbones, but my proteinuria stopped. Glomerulonephritis (inflammation of the kidney from streptococcal infection, often as a sequel to tonsillitis) was very common. We learned about the benefits of penicillin in this illness. Not too many antibiotics were available besides penicillin, streptomycin, chloromycetin, and sulfa. In those days, pneumonia was easily cured with small doses of penicillin. Community health was just being conceived in India, and its cost effectiveness was being considered. We were taught a considerable amount about cardiac disease. We saw many patients with myocardial infarction. Heart attack was very common because of diet, sedentary habits, and because many persons of the Indian subcontinent have small coronary arteries. We also saw various forms of dysrythmias (abnormality of heart rhythm). We saw patients with valvular (valves of the heart) disease caused also by the same organism that causes tonsillitis. I recall once waking up in the bed of a young patient with leukemia. I had passed out while standing next to his bedside when his prognosis was being discussed in English. In those days, no one survived five years with that diagnosis. He did not understand English, but he helped me to lie down. I remember the embarrassed face of a young resident in Ohio when the professor chided him for expressing a similar lack of sensitivity. He had made a negative comment in English in front of a cancer patient of Hispanic origin.

In 1969, I joined the neurological surgery program at Ohio State University where Dr. William E. Hunt was the chairman. Dr. Charles Wilson had accepted me in the California program. He found out that he could not train me. Although I was perfectly qualified, I had a stigma: I was foreign-born. He had chosen me after a thorough interview in which his colleagues had participated as well. However, God is merciful. In spite of the discrimination by the state of California, he helped me to be trained by one of the finest surgeons in the world. I did not realize that it was discrimination until recently. My father had taught me to accept rejection willfully as a part of life.

The neurosurgical training was rather rigorous. We practically spent two years in the hospital. Four years of training were required to be eligible to take the first part of the neurosurgical board examination. The neurosurgical training was not just physically demanding but emotionally draining as well. There was a constant challenge on our intellectual ability to function under dire stress. I took some extra courses in anatomy, psychology, and physiology, and worked many hours in the laboratory to get a master's degree in anatomy by going to school on the days that I was off duty. I had originally planned to get a Ph.D. in anatomy, but it became impossible because of my attitude toward a particular professor of anatomy who had a bigoted attitude. His insulting comments toward my rather successful accomplishment in the tests led me to react in a manner that was not conducive to getting a satisfactory grade. I just could not overcome my negative attitude toward him. I basically lost the drive that I have always had within me and could not persevere.

My father had told me sometime before that there would be a few who will love me for my color and there would be others who will like me despite my color. I was glad that a few did not like me for my color. It helped me to realize that the God that made the horses made the donkeys as well, and there was room for both to graze in America. My professor had arranged to pay for this extra schooling because I could not afford it. This failure, of course, did not affect my functioning as a neurosurgical trainee. I believe it taught me to understand how pervasive discrimination is within the education system, even among some so-called educated people of the northern part of the country. The situation bothered me quite a bit at times when I was alone. I knew that it would be difficult to succeed, being a first-generation immigrant. But I had a second strike against me—I had color. I liked my color, although at times I wished I didn't have it. I chose the second alternative. I worked harder than my colleagues did. I wanted to be more successful than the rest. This type of competitive spirit placed extra pressure on me. It was, indeed, truly burdensome at times! My family held a privileged position in the society for seven generations. Now I was getting a taste of being on the other side.

During the training period, I wrote numerous papers, and some of them got published in the medical journals. My professor told me that American scientific writing should be factual and not flowery. He suggested I read *Elements of Style* by William Strunk. He also thought I should read some of the writings of Samuel Johnson, English poet, essayist and lexicographer, for entertainment and also to understand the distinction between the two types of prose. We laughed as I recited what I thought was Johnson's request for a pinch of snuff: "Let me introduce my digiterial extremities into your odoriferous concavity and extract a few pulverized atoms of tobacco which on entering my nostrils would give me tantalizing pleasure."

During these years, I spent so much time in the hospital that I couldn't come home to take my wife to the hospital when we had our first child. I came home soon after she had delivered to find a smiling mother and a crying baby as soon as I entered the house. Being utterly bewildered at the situation, I called the operator in the hospital and asked her to page me. My wife, lying in a pool of blood, consoled me. She reminded me that I was already there and did not need to be paged. Soon after that, my professor came in with ten other physicians he had gathered on the way because he hadn't delivered a baby in many years. They took my wife to the hospital to deliver the placenta. I sat in her room for a short period, embarrassed. I was a failure again. Soon an emergency rescued me.

Da had not read Henry James and did not know *The Pension Beauregard* and, therefore, the concept, "To do the best, to know the best—to have, to desire, to recognize only the best" did not exist. This part of the American concept of living became a part of my life later as I scurried along to meet multiple deadlines during the rest of my days of active practice. I made six o'clock morning rounds, which was followed by seven-thirty operating room, and then performed myelograms (a procedure to check the spinal column with injection of dye) in between cases. There were consultations to be seen and dictations to be completed. These activities were punctuated by conversations with my secretary, as well as with colleagues who referred patients. I needed time to talk to the patients and their families. In addition to this work, I had to make an occasional visit to the emergency room. There was always a committee or staff meeting during part of the evenings in one of the hospitals. I missed many dinners at home, and, on several occasions, the whole family traveled with me from hospital to hospital while I examined patients in different emergency rooms. I never asked them about their day, as though the whole universe revolved around me. Such was the routine of the day.

Despite my learning to manage time wisely and effectively, I realized that I could not stretch the day to twenty-eight hours. It was only later that I heard from my children that their mother told them to be quiet when I would arrive home, because they thought that I would be intolerant and impatient. I did not have time for the very people who loved me the most, and they were afraid of me. As much as I would like to believe that was not true, my behavior perhaps reflected that I was less tolerant of my family. I took it for granted that they would accept this attitude and I could continue to behave in this manner with impunity, owing to the fact I was trying to make a living.

A sense of denial enveloped me, and the shell had no eyeholes for me to see through it. I continued studying, writing papers, and attending parties wearing funny black-tie outfits and participating in small talk. I was engrossed in working long hours for the relentless pursuit of being a successful neurosurgeon. My family worked around me. It was as if I were some kind of a deity that needed to be flattered and pleased constantly so that some calamity or grave consequence would not befall them. I was in a trap—the trap of pleasure—a trap where there is no satiation—a trap where my patients thought I was wonderful—and I gloated in that. It was a trap that blinded me to the slow, cancerous death I was living. I was the "Tyger, tyger, burning bright/In the forests of the night" ("The Tiger," William Blake). Everybody knew the temper that was lurking in there, so everyone who loved me was on guard.

I grew out of this elusive rat race to be successful as I grew older. I learned that if I did anything with love and patience, it is lot more meaningful than to do my best in a state of complete fatigue. I conquered the pleasure of conquest! I surrendered to my soul and God, and asked for His help to make me whole. Do you know what it might feel like in the pit of your stomach if a child in a go-cart tried to race across the fast lane in front of your speeding car? I was in this car of life, driving merrily with my sunglasses on. I braked and got out and only saw the cart at first. It is only after I looked further that I saw my soul still safe, held in the cushion of a puddle of water on the concrete road. I understood God's miracle. I slowed down to accept his blessings. I sang, "I once was lost, but now am found/Was blind, but now I see."

My mental status epilepticus was ameliorated, my insomnia improved, and I had peace when I decided to retread my life. There is a fundamental difference between obedience and surrendering. When I surrendered, it was a positive act, and there was no opportunity for disobedience. I was blind and extended my hand, and God took it to guide me where I belonged. I was granted a new energy that was to be redirected in a manner to make my life more meaningful. The pressure of performance seemed to go away. The sense of achieving became less important, and the new work became a source of lasting pleasure, even when the act was over. I realized that the only thing that I was successful at during my twenty-five years of practice was in driving myself crazy to a point that I did not think about anything else but work. My entire life was work oriented, and I needed to change my work to be life oriented and certainly family oriented. I had no time for lovemaking; I only had raw sex for self-gratification without giving my wife the love and tenderness she needed and most certainly deserved.

I had forgotten Emily Dickinson's lines:

Success is counted sweetest
By those who ne'er succeed.

• • • • •

At Ohio State University, I observed and assisted in many difficult procedures. I learned by observing the outstanding bedside manners of my professor. I also noticed his charm and charisma, qualities necessary to be successful in the practice of medicine. He demonstrated by his behavior the honesty and integrity that is essential to have a guilt-free conscience. I believe that made him sleep well during the few hours that were available to him. He expected the best from us, and he also engendered a spirit of learning. He induced within us the spirit to drive the engine necessary to survive in this stressful field. He imparted knowledge by constantly challenging us. I tried to remain like a sponge and absorbed as much as possible during my training period. He was a true teacher in every sense. His compassion and truthfulness toward his patients were sincere. There was always mutual love and respect between him and his patients. He taught me to be practical and to avoid unnecessary tests. I got the distinct impression from him that honesty and a relationship with the patients were more important than worrying about litigation.

Many years later, I operated on a patient's neck from the front. He was an older gentleman who had become clumsy and spastic. I was not absolutely sure if he was developing early symptoms of Lou Gehrig's disease, or whether most of the symptoms of spasticity were related to pressure from arthritis in his neck. I had explained to his wife that the former was not correctable. It would lead to death by pneumonia or such, and that sometimes the two conditions coexist. I operated on him. I took several X-rays in the operating room to be sure that I removed the bone from the correct levels.

However, I realized in the recovery room after taking another X-ray that I didn't do the exact operation I had intended to perform. I shared that with the family immediately. Next morning, when my patient was of clear mind and fully awake from the ill effects of anesthesia, I told him that I had performed an incorrect operation. I said that I would like to correct it if he wished and that I was sorry. At that time, he held my hand and thanked me for being truthful and felt that he would like to see what happens. His wound healed, and he recovered from the surgery. After about one year, he started getting progressively worse and was diagnosed by another physician to have amyotrophic lateral sclerosis (Lou Gehrig's disease). I received a phone call from a veteran's hospital that they were considering a tracheostomy.

The family didn't want any procedure performed on him unless I felt it was indicated. I discussed it with the family, and we decided against it. I felt blessed by his trust in me even at his death! I prayed for more humility.

• • • • •

Dr. W. E. Hunt had classified aneurysms of the brain according to the survival rate, and, as such, the risks of surgery if the condition was operated on within a certain time frame. He was a master surgeon using the available tools of the trade of that period. I assisted him in an operation in 1969 that took him about twelve or thirteen hours to complete. He removed a meningioma (tumor of the covering of the brain) with the help of a microscope. The tumor had covered the nerves of the eye. It was adherent to the structures around the pituitary gland (an enplaque meningioma arising from the planum sphenoidale) and the carotid artery. The patient became completely well. It made such an impression on me that in 1992 (twenty-five years later), when I had an opportunity to operate on a similar case, I remembered every detail of his technique. I wrote him a letter thanking him for teaching me. These days we have lasers and CUSA (ultrasonic sound) and better microscopes in our armamentarium to assist us. The patient of mine was almost blind before the operation but recovered considerably. He did not have any insurance, but he wanted to do something for me. He mowed my lawn for one summer, and we considered it an even trade. He has referred several patients to me subsequently. This reminded me of the trading relationship my father had with most of his patients.

I have been pleasantly surprised to walk into my waiting room to find a cage full of live chickens that one of my patients brought to express her satisfaction for my services. I have been flattered and humbled by the expression of love from many of my patients. There have been some who brought gifts of dressed rabbits, squirrels, and fresh honey in the combs. These loving gestures and the kind words of many of the patients have given me the true incentive to work and have made my life more meaningful.

It became apparent that the tide was changing in regard to the method of payment by insurance companies for the services rendered by physicians. The insurance companies and attorneys were sending many persons to me for second opinions and independent medical evaluations. This type of referral was more prevalent in cases of litigation related to workmen's compensation benefits. I had never called or asked anyone for referral. I believe my conservative attitude in addition to my credentials attracted attention. Whenever there was a conflict with the treating surgeons, the insurance company accepted my opinion; thus I was becoming the pariah of the aggressive, young operating surgeons although the senior surgeons in the community respected my opinion. At times, what bothered me the most was the fact that they disliked me more than my opinion, because they took my opinion personally.

Collegiality was at its lowest ebb. I felt I was being dissected in the hallways of the hospital through useless vituperations by economically challenged surgeons. As I earned the nickname of the "insurance doctor," it was implied that I was the villain. I felt that every time I saw someone for consultation, I needed to submit myself to his or her blade of justice, as though I embodied a proud, disdainful, and hardened malefactor. In these situations, I thought of "my favorite things" so I did not feel sad anymore. I comforted myself knowing that at least I wasn't a Protestant heretic of the pre-Elizabethan era. I realized that no act creates more enemies than an act of giving an opinion that affects the pocketbook of someone else. I felt that nothing creates more envy than being young and successful in the eyes of the people who are unable to share in the joy of a neighbor. I chose to create the smoke screen of the latter perception. I let them wallow in their jealous dissatisfaction while I taught at Cambridge, England, and listened to the electrifying music of "Saturday Night Fever" in London at the Palladium. I often wondered if they would have disliked me as much if I had lacked color! It is shameful, but I think I liked myself even more at this point, not as much due to my success as because I was able to create a deception in the weaker minds with no effort.

I thanked God for blessing me with another opportunity. This teaching assignment was much like a gift from heaven, because I didn't anticipate it.

I began to enjoy the challenge. I believed in my approach and in the principle that a good surgeon knows when to operate but a better surgeon knows in addition to that when not to operate. More important, this gave me an opportunity to read more, which allowed me to provide appropriate references supporting my opinions. Many of the people bearing grudges were less than pleased at my new style, as these reports became more difficult to dispute. Somehow efforts of intimidation and economic coercion always bring out the best in me. My practice doubled as I harnessed all my energy to provide even better service of reporting my opinions in a more prompt manner.

I could go away to work as a volunteer, during which time I operated almost daily. I would return to a full schedule of patient evaluations in my office, particularly during the days when a large number of physicians were having a dwindling practice. I praised God for this great opportunity that He bestowed upon me without my ever having to ask for it. I worked harder and enjoyed having this new responsibility of a larger practice. This situation was very useful to me psychologically, as well as financially.

I acknowledged the financial windfall as a gift. I made

a concerted effort to give away all my profits every year to local and international charities. I felt more blessed as I followed this path of progressive renunciation. Now, I realized what my grandfather and father said about money based on their religious beliefs. "For the love of money is the root of all evil" (1 Timothy 6:10) became clear to me. I understood that money was a necessity but not the love of it. The saying from the Upanishad about being a fish and swimming in the water and learning to dodge the sharks to survive and, at the same time, not allowing the water to stick to my body made immense sense to me. I grew up.

I decided many years ago that I would honor my mother by setting up trusts for research in her name or by setting up scholarships to help the disadvantaged in every country where I work. I was given the opportunity to do just that over the years, which has brought me immense joy. I prayed. I asked God to give me the ability and the willingness to give away most of my income besides what I needed for retirement. I wanted God to help me conquer greed. I asked Him to give me the opportunity to show my appreciation to all those who have made my journey easier.

Once a group of physicians asked me to be a financially involved member. They were starting a project that involved building a CT scan and MRI facility for referring their own patients. This, they thought, would be more profitable than referring the patient to a hospital. I would have been a good referral source owing to my successful practice. I was threatened with "no referral" from this group for my discomfort with and inaction in this endeavor. Unfortunately, for these adventurous investors, recently the government (the ubiquitous Medicare) has disallowed such investment opportunities through self-referral. I learned that some people didn't like me for being successful. There were others who just didn't like me to be correct, especially when I had suggested the possibility of conflict of interest. That I had the audacity not to sign up as an investor was considered an affront. I was afraid to join because the investors could have been exposed as greedy.

I continued to disagree on multiple fusion of the spine on patients without any objective neurological findings or objective evidence of instability. I have avoided admonitions such as "if it hurts, don't do it." Instead, I recommend exercises. I believe oversolicitiousness on the part of the family can prolong illness at times. I thought that it was almost impossible for someone to need bilateral carpal tunnel, bilateral pronator teres, ulnar nerve, and thoracic outlet operations after working at General Electric making dishwashers for a while. I felt that on many occasions if we scale down our expectations, we could be more functional. I am convinced that counseling and rehabilitation are more helpful and important in treating chronic pain than removal of an incidental disk finding on the MRI scan.

There have been times when the patients were less than satisfied with me because of my disapproval of a prospective surgery that was recommended.

On a number of occasions, I was threatened by statements such as "my back may not be working, but my trigger finger still works." The insurance company investigators photographed one such person. He left my office wearing a brace and walked with a cane, but he drove more than one hundred miles to set up a hot dog stand for a ball game in West Virginia. It seemed he found it convenient to use the cane to hold up a tarpaulin to cover the roof of the stand. He climbed on an elevated bench during the process of setting up shop.

On one occasion, a person came to see me who had a cranioplasty (plastic replacement of part of the skull) subsequent to a head injury sustained in an automobile accident. He stated that the cranioplasty talked to him when he "gets in the mood" and that deterred him from functioning as proficiently as he had prior to the accident. He thought that the white doctors had conspired against him, and his lawyer had sent him to me because I was less white. I was pleased to know that I was not thought of as "less than white" and felt honored to be in the newly designated class. I informed him that he needed to see a different type of a head doctor, one who cures people by talking and not by cutting!

I have wrestled with the issues of secondary gain, lack of education, job satisfaction, and job availability in determining the seriousness of work-related injury as perceived by the patients. This is particularly important when back pain is not associated with any objective findings. Above all, I have always given the patients the benefit of the doubt in regard to the symptoms, but my treatment recommendations have always been based on objective findings. I have expressed opinion based on thorough understanding of the literature. I have tried not to tilt the balance with undue optimism toward my own perceived talent in relation to others. I have learned to be sensitive; for example, now I say someone weighs 160 pounds and is five feet two inches tall rather than use the negative word "obese." I think that with the present fiscal constraints, it is imperative that we base our recommendations on sound evidence so that we can say that "it will happen" rather than "it might happen." The days of "since it hurts, let's take it out and see" are gone, and we have certainly learned that from all the gallbladders and uteruses that have been discarded for just being there and were "possibly" causing pain.

Several of my relatives were attorneys. My father told me a few stories about the attorneys. A physician, an engineer, and an attorney were trying to decide whose profession was the oldest. The doctor claimed that creation of Eve from Adam's rib was a surgical challenge in the days with minimal tools, and that's when it all started. The engineer, on the other hand, had a clever idea. He felt that the world was in chaos before the creation, and the process of bringing it to an organized pattern was an engineering maneuver. More important, it was a necessary step before God would even consider the creation. Therefore, his profession was older. The doctor accepted the argument as being reasonable. The attorney pondered for a while. He said that his profession, then, must be the oldest because there must have been someone to create the chaos!

One of my uncles was a public prosecutor. As a young boy, I had seen him struggle with difficult cases. One time, when I was about ten or so, I remember seeing pictures of dismembered human body parts in his briefcase when he was getting ready for a trial. He didn't want to show them to me, so I chose to see them when he was sleeping. I didn't understand why I would not be allowed to see those, and yet so many people in the courtroom could see them. He studied my father's anatomy books and determined that the perpetrator had to be a doctor, because all the bones were cut exactly through the joints. Therefore, no one could hear the hacking of bones. There were no witnesses available who could testify to having heard any noise of butchering or such. He proved his case. This doctor in Calcutta was put in jail for life. We had a celebration in our house with whiskey and a great feast. I was allowed to partake in the celebration. My involvement was only in the latter event. On such occasions, usually after all the congratulations were finished, we had an opportunity to either read from something interesting or we could say something clever. My uncle was considerably older than my dad was, and he read from

Rabindranath's "Gitanjali":

> On the day when death will knock at thy door, what wilt thou offer to him? Oh, I will set before my guest the full vessel of my life—I will never let him go with empty hands.
>
> All the sweet vintage of all my autumn days and summer nights, all the earnings and gleanings of my busy life will I place before him at the close of my days when death will knock at my door.

Usually, the occasions were not so somber as this one. Here, a doctor was involved, and several innocent people were killed, which I thought led everyone to talk about his own mortality. My father always believed death was a part of life, and he had said to me once that we cannot prepare for our own birth, but we should prepare for our death. He thought it was always easy for the person who died, but the preparation was necessary for the people who must continue to live. He paid a lot of respect to the time necessary for grieving. It was customary in India to host a feast after a few days when someone died. This was symbolic to suggest that the mourning time was over, and the mourners were grateful for everyone's support during the difficult times. My father thought that this was a big waste of money. He didn't like the idea of feeding a bunch of people when he wouldn't be here to participate. He chose instead to have many feasts when he was alive. He liked the flowers when he could smell them rather than when they would be "wasted while lying on a wilted body," my father often said.

• • • • •

It wasn't until 1988 that I started working in Brazil. It turned out to be a great opportunity to make new friends and be in a completely different environment all by myself again. I did not speak any Portuguese at all. Dr. A. DaSilva and I have become close friends since then. We were able to participate in a considerable amount of academic work besides the daily clinical work of doctoring. Here we performed head operations using Black & Decker drills. This was just as effective as using the fancy, expensive drills I use at home. It gave me an opportunity for the first time since my training to check my malleability and the ability to improvise. Subsequently, I have gone back to Brazil and set up a stereotactic (computer-based operation through a small hole) system for brain operations. I treated some illnesses similar to what I treat in the United States. In addition, I also saw cysticercosis (worm from the pigs) and echinococcus (worm from the sheep). I noticed that the doctors have separate waiting rooms for rich people and for the "others." I learned about their billing systems, as well as about their medical facilities, which are little different from ours.

• • • • •

America is truly unique and is for the people, and it becomes more and more evident as I travel. I also believe the progress we are making toward equality is also quite rapid in relation to most other places I have been so far. However, I believe because we are Americans, we are not satisfied. We cannot rest on our laurels until our system is truly free and equal for everyone.

On one of the days that I did not have any work, I visited the great Iguaçú Falls (world's largest waterfall) bordering Argentina. I worked in the state of Paraná, which is extremely fertile, and while there, visited a large farm and learned about their agricultural techniques and how they use waste products. They are very enterprising and innovative. They have crossbred a Brahmin cow with a Simmental, which can make more milk and survive in arid areas of Brazil. Probably the most important crop is sugarcane, and it is used to make sugar and alcohol. The alcohol is the main fuel for the automobiles. The leftover sugarcane by-product, called *baggas*, is used for building fires to heat homes. I found the people most friendly. I actively participated in sharing the joy of friendship by tasting and toasting with beer. During my multiple visits, I believe we learned from each other regarding different ways of thinking. We have improved our surgical techniques to help some of the people of Brazil regarding back, neck, and head problems.

The Presbyterian church I visited in Londrina is much like the Baptist churches at home in regard to the singing. The culture of the congregation shows a lot of animation. There seemed to be a lot of arms raising and swaying during singing. I thought also that it was a great idea to project the music on the wall. It saved on the expense of the hymnbooks in a country with limited resources.

We participated in national studies to determine the efficacy of radiation treatment in brain tumors while I was at Ohio State University. We also had a grant to study spinal cord injuries during my residency period. Dr. R. White at the Cleveland Clinic had determined that some monkeys had gained neurological function after their spinal cord was cooled rapidly after a traumatic event. We tried that on about twenty-two humans, with dismal results. I, along with my colleagues, became very proficient in performing multilevel laminectomy (removal of the bone covering the spinal cord) with utmost dispatch. Subsequent to removal of the bone, we stood in the operating room often for more than eight hours washing the spinal cord with ice cold water. During these times, I often made judgmental comments without the benefit of scientific research. Dr. Hunt taught us intellectual honesty by stating the failure of a well-tried project when it was time to publish a report about it. I developed a special interest in treating spinal cord problems during the process.

In the late seventies, I had an opportunity to see a thirty-five-year-old woman with a very difficult arteriovenous (abnormal blood vessels) malformation of the spinal cord near the base of the brain, which could not be corrected by conventional surgery. I read almost everything I could find on the subject and then decided to inject crazy glue inside the blood vessels selectively to seal the small blood vessels shut so that they could not continue to shunt blood away from the spinal cord and produce paralysis. This was the first time such surgery was being performed in Louisville, and she had already obtained different opinions. After reading some of the research that Dr. A. Berenstein was doing in New York, I thought I could help her. I had learned catheter techniques while I was a resident.

After six different attempts, we were able to achieve our goal, and she has remained a functional person as of today. Dr. Berenstein has performed another procedure more recently since a recurrence after fifteen years.

• • • • •

I am particularly pleased with the intensive care unit at Nepal where many different services can use the facility for the benefit of the patients. Here I was pleased to be involved with Dr. M. Bagan, who organized the neurosurgical program at the teaching hospital. This is a developing department where many doctors from the United States have contributed. I have seen patients who have traveled on the back of another person on mountainous roads for two days. They had to spend another day in a bus before they could arrive at the clinic. Many of the conditions become quite advanced by the time the patients arrived for our care, and many of the patients go away without getting investigated. They are apprehensive of the presumed expense, which on most occasions is minimal. The hospital has recently obtained a CT scanner, which will improve the service immensely. I have operated on multiple patients who have sustained fractured spine after falling off the mountains. I have treated children afflicted with brain abscesses that had developed subsequent to ear infections. I have participated in treatment of patients infected with the tuberculosis of the spine. I have enjoyed being part of such a friendly group that supported our work. I had wanted to visit Tibet ever since I was a child. I found an opportunity while working here.

I took a trip to Tibet last year to see the land of the Dalai Lama. I traveled by bus from Kathmandu. As we neared the border, a landslide delayed us by about four hours. However, I walked around it. It took us four days to reach Lhasa by traveling in a car. Here, I visited several monasteries and learned about the lifestyle of the Buddhist monks. There was peace in the air. I felt soothed by the chanting of the holy words. The effects of the Chinese occupation are obvious among the general population. They appear more subdued than I would imagine from the religious teaching alone. I had a discussion with some people about the possibility of Jesus having visited the Himis monastery during the time he was between fourteen and twenty-seven years old (*Lost Years of Jesus* by Elizabeth Prophet, Summit Bea, 1988). I enjoyed the lively discourse about Swami Abhidananda. I learned about Roerich's visit to Himis and

Professor Max Muller's skepticism about the subject. I planned to visit the Himis monastery someday on my own.

I work as a volunteer in Nepal now, and even now the cultural milieu does not allow a doctor to ask about epilepsy directly and we have to be very circumspect about it. I saw a young lady who had a genuine convulsion that I diagnosed from the description of her spell. However, we had to ask questions in a manner that would not offend her and then performed a CT scan of the brain. We found calcifications suggesting the graveyard of many worms, a condition known as cysticercosis. This is a common malady afflicting many individuals who are exposed to oro-fecal contamination that occurs by eating vegetables grown with fresh night soil as the main soil nutrient. This is also possibly transmitted from infected pork, but most people in this area do not indulge in porcine pleasure. As a matter of fact, it is only recently that I have noticed shops in India that serve wonton soup.

My assignment in Peru was in the Segundo Social Hospital. Here everyone spoke Castiliano (Spanish), so I learned a bit of Spanish before I went. I met one of the physicians at Lima and then subsequently went over to Arequipa. This is a beautiful town of white stones and a volcano. Misti is its most conspicuous inhabitant. I still remember that the first time I went there to operate. The microscope shook a little bit during the operation, and they called it a seismo (earthquake). Everyone continued without blinking an eye. I being from Louisville and not having experienced an earthquake before was most conspicuous vocally. Here I taught the students. I made rounds with the doctors. I also operated on some patients. I mostly enjoyed visiting the Colca Canyon. I watched the condors fly. I walked the Inca trail to visit Machu Picchu, the castle of the Incas. I have treated patients from Puno. I visited Lake Titicaca, the highest navigated lake in the world. The head operations were still performed with the drills that we used in the early sixties when I arrived for the first time, but now we have managed to get the drills they need to make the operations faster. In Peru, they have three-tiered care, and those with money get the most prompt care in private hospitals. I also worked at Chiclayo, in northern Peru. They have fine instruments there, and the surgical skill of my colleagues is very high indeed. The graves of Señor Sipan have been dug out and he is considered the King Tut of South America. *Cabrito* (goat meat) is a delicacy of this area, whereas *camarones* (shrimp) is the "must have" of Arequipa. It is superfluous to say that I indulged myself in all the gastronomical delicacies to the fullest as I washed them down with an abundace of Arequipina, Crystal, and Antarctica (fine local beers). Drs. H. Aragon and C. Uriarte have been most gracious to me and have made every effort to introduce me to the Peruvian neurosurgery. Dr. A. Pineda is our American counterpart who has been instrumental in arranging our mutual learning opportunity in Peru.

• • • • •

We ran a very busy trauma center at Ohio State University. It was not unusual for us to see two or three patients with serious trauma per night. These patients were transported by helicopter and often arrived in the hospital in a comatose state.

Many of them arrived while having their heart massaged by a six foot two inch tall doctor. The accompanying nurse of smaller stature standing next to him usually appeared totally bathed in human blood. The doctor in charge of the helicopter had just returned from Vietnam. I (very inexperienced and quick to make a judgment) often thought that he still had not had his fill of blood. He might have needed a fresh reminder of Hanoi every so often for a sanguineous satisfaction. I realized soon that it was my fatigue that blamed him for his heroic yet altruistic efforts. They always called the neurosurgical resident at the end of this drama. It was presumed that we had the power owing to human ingenuity to revive a long-dead person who had a flicker on the EKG machine.

At the center, we treated many patients with gunshot injury. The other most common group of patients was involved in automobile accidents. One of my greatest learning experiences was when we had to treat a young child who had lost a significant amount of her scalp. She was thrown out of a car that was involved in an accident. This child was not allowed to have a human skin graft because of the religious belief of the family. I personally was rather angry, to say the least. I argued with the family for hours. Eventually, there was a discussion to get a pig skin graft (from the laboratory), as this was acceptable. I saw the child for a final visit with our service after six months. The child underwent multiple plastic surgical procedures. The details about grafting procedures have skipped my mind. I was surprised that the head wound had healed just fine.

I became a tolerant individual regarding such situations subsequently. I studied about the belief in question and attended their church service to learn more about the faith. Subsequently, during my practice I have been rather conservative about the use of blood during the procedures. However, in some countries, such as Nepal, India, and Africa, blood is used lot more liberally and the incidence of blood-related complications is obviously much higher.

About twenty years ago, I saw a young girl (ten years old) who had a very large tumor inside the ventricle (cavity) of the brain. During the discussion and planning of the operation, it became apparent that the parents didn't believe in blood transfusion, even if it meant death for their daughter. I suggested they go elsewhere. However, eventually I operated on the child at their insistence. The first operation lasted six hours. When I thought that the child might die from the continuing blood loss, I closed the wound and informed the family. She was my daughter's age, and I could not let her die in my hand, knowing that there was an alternative. I waited for eight weeks and removed the tumor with a laser with the help of my friend Dr. S. Natelson from Knoxville. I discussed her case with Dr. C. Wilson from California prior to the second operation on the tumor. He had suggested that we might consider radiation to reduce the vascularity of the tumor and thus the subsequent blood loss during the proposed operation. I discussed with her family the fact that her growth would be almost certainly stunted because of the harmful effect of the radiation on her pituitary and hypothalamus circuit at such a young age. Her postoperative hemoglobin (iron carrying oxygen) was six grams (normal for her age is fourteen). She is doing fine, and I am greatly indebted to the family for trusting me. She had a giant cell tumor. She has had no recurrence. Subsequent to the first operation, she has needed a shunt (placement of a tube to reduce increased pressure). She has graduated from high school with honors. Now she is almost as tall as her mother after being treated with growth hormone for four years.

I was involved in one medical malpractice suit over the years of my practice when my insurance company paid out a small sum of money. The trauma of being sued is quite significant. I had left a small piece of cotton underneath the skin of a person's back after performing a successful operation. This was removed without much of a problem. It caused her no harm. She was pleased with the settlement, and subsequently referred several patients to me. This was a stressful event. As soon as I recognized the situation, which was about six months later, I informed her about the problem. I told her that the count in the operating room was correct but obviously not accurate. She seemed to understand the difference and that was that. I told her that I would notify my insurance company, which collects premiums for protection against such mishaps, and I was sincerely sorry.

I had access to consultations about the diseases of my patients from several neurosurgeons in the world. Therefore, I often called upon my friends to discuss difficult cases. At times, I sent them the X-rays to get their opinions. Most of my patients liked the fact that I carried out the footwork and that I cared enough to get an opinion from another person. I found it very helpful. I saw a young lady about one year after she was involved in a serious automobile accident, sustaining multiple fractures about the face and head. She had developed dripping of a clear fluid from her nose whenever she went out on a date. She was led to believe that a head operation would be necessary to close the leak of spinal fluid that may be running down her nose. After detailed checking, I felt that this was not spinal fluid. This was a condition called alligator's tears that can occur on rare occasions from aberrant connections of nerves after an injury.

I discussed this case with Dr. C. Wilson in California. He suggested that we try atropine nose drops. We also asked her to avoid jalapeño peppers in pizzas. Her tearing from the nose stopped, and she didn't need a head operation.

We are a lot more worried about the postoperative hemoglobin in the West than in some of the other countries where I work. Many patients in some of the other countries have very low hemoglobin preoperatively, but come out of the operation just fine. I had an opportunity to treat a nineteen-year-old girl in Nepal who was almost paralyzed in all four limbs owing to the odontoid process (the bone just below the head from the back) being pushed against the upper part of the spinal cord due to softening from tuberculosis. I was able to remove this bone from the base of the brain by operating through a small opening in the palate. We fused her neck at the same time, using part of her hipbone, and wired them together. She also needed a tracheotomy. She was treated with antituberculosis treatment for nine months. After one year, she was well and working. She had very low hemoglobin at the time of the operation, but she was treated with iron orally for six months to combat the anemia.

I have had the opportunity to work in Zimbabwe with men like Dr. L. Levy. He has taught me to evaluate the patients in a manner that is most conducive to good patient care in that particular environment. I have learned to treat and feel while performing neurosurgery under circumstances much different than in the United States. He has taught me about faith. He has helped me to use the available methods of survival where more than fifteen percent of the people are afflicted with HIV virus. He has helped me to be tolerant.

Once, I was operating under less than adequate illumination because the assigned person for the job of changing bulbs was not available. I was not allowed to change the lightbulb as that would have been considered to be against the standard protocol. It took me four hours to perform an operation that I could have finished in two. I have worked with nurses who have translated for me and made the communication easier between the patients and me. There were days when I examined thirty-five patients or so in one day. Many of them had traveled more than two days in a bus for this appointment, only to be admitted in a ward with no beds. They were assigned floor beds. The antiquated system prevents the staff from working overtime. This often leads to backlogging of work that translates to patients staying in the hospital sometimes for a month before getting an operation. Usually, by that time, the condition is considerably worse than at the time of admission. The nurses have shared with me the frustrations of working under trying circumstances, particularly with the spine patients. No rehabilitation facilities are available. The majority of spine injury patients die within a year after going home from some complication of urinary tract infection or pneumonia. Patients with meningitis stay in the same room with the others including those with meningo-myelocele (a birth defect with open spine) owing to lack of isolation facilities. There is shortage of running water throughout the week. Cursory handwashing was performed on the days "of the water." The towel we used for drying the hands possibly acted as a culture medium. Simple devices such as cervical (neck) collars are not generally available to poor people. CT scans are available to the patients only after several days of waiting. The equipment in private hospitals is much better. It seemed that the treatment proceeded much faster under these special circumstances. I have prayed for my patients before operating on them. I believe that prayer has played an important role in their successful recovery.

During the weekends while working in Africa, I traveled to Hwange National Park. I saw the Victoria Falls as well. The true beauty of the elephant in the wilderness is depicted here at its best. The younger of the group stay in the middle, protected by the older animals. These mammoths walk in herds and are rarely alone. They stand tall and firm as the giant tusks of hard ivory protrude upward and forward as though they are getting ready to play the trumpet. The big ears fan and cool them while they observe the visitor. Then, while eating and walking, they all follow the leader through the open grassland. Weakling trees are trampled down with a crackling sound, as they become the mulch floors of the prairies. About fifty thousand elephants reside there. The poachers target their attractive dentition as the solution to the economic hardship in Africa, although in reality it is merely a windfall to a few. For the elephants, there is even a bigger problem, even if they escape these illegal bullets. Men armed with the stamp of legal authority shoot them lest they become too successful in their breeding while participating in a tumultuous foreplay. I did not like the word culling, because it seemed like a cunning method of legalized killing. I understood that such a license is sold at times when these animals have become too many! The gigantic moisture cloud of the Victoria Falls brought a welcome relief from the hot African sun while I sipped on some cold beer, pondering which species might decimate us as we become too many in their perception.

The monkeys at the Tiger Tops in Nepal live a quiet and protected life from the aggressiveness of men. They munch and twitter and jump from tree to tree while observing and warning from their elevated vista. I remember once being on the back of an elephant for two days as we looked for a tiger.

As we stood on a hill, we saw at a distance sambars grazing in a small pasture next to tall elephant grass. The sky was clear, and the afternoon sun was just getting ready to call it a day. There were long shadows of the grass on a small patch of water filled with cattails, with few strands of clouds standing still in between the shimmering shadows of this limpid water. There was not even a breeze, and even the mosquitoes didn't open their wings fully to honor the moment. They aspirated quietly at their nearest landing site. Everything looked perfectly innocent. But within this image of innocence was the camouflaged body of the revered tiger who seemed to be on the prowl, or was it just taking a siesta? I thought of William Blake's line in "The Tyger," "Did he who made the Lamb make thee?" Nevertheless, it was barely visible, but mesmerizing, fierce eyes betrayed its intent. There was pin-drop silence in the forest. Everybody seemed to know that there was a kill in progress. It seemed even the leaves were watching quietly, as though they might have to testify as witnesses. I held my breath as I gazed at a distance to see the swift striped feline stealthily advance toward the herd, its unsuspecting prey. It advanced so quietly that nothing moved on the forest floor while its eyes remained fixed to the target. Suddenly, something happened. The silence was sliced. The big racked sambar looked up. I realized that the wind, the friend of the sambar, had shifted. The monkeys chattered in joy. All I could hear was the galloping of the hooves and the gloating and giggling of the leaves. The hunt was over for Sher Khan. Sambar, 1, and Sher Khan, 0. Later, I came back to the camp to nurse the burning blister on my seat, caused by the prolonged ride on the back of the elephant. I believe it had popped during a moment of excitement when I had joined in the clapping of my hands with the cheering monkeys. I slapped the slobbering mosquito on my cheek to interrupt its meal, as it was time for intermission from this engaging drama of nature.

· · · · ·

I lived in northern Wisconsin for a while, where I practiced in a large clinic and lived on a farm. I raised a hog named Arnold, much like in "Green Acres," who became quite a pet for the family. He followed my girl when she walked around in the field. Arnold oinked when he wanted to be scratched. My daughter had a horse, April, who liked to stay outside even when the temperature was forty below zero. I would bring her in the barn to get rid of the ice from her hooves with a screwdriver. This would help her not to fall down if she were to run to warm up a little bit when cold!

I also raised about a hundred chickens. They always followed me when I opened the barn door. I raised these from little chicks under a heat lamp after they had arrived in a box in the mail. I enjoyed being the pied piper, carrying the bucket of grain while an entourage of chickens followed me. I felt powerful. I was greatly uplifted by these chicks at a time when I needed cheering up the most. Usually at the end of the day, I was often fatigued and unhappy—more so at those times when the operation hadn't gone the way I had anticipated. I always rewarded the hungry poultry with a large number of vitamin pills that were given to me as samples by the medical representatives. My girl always had to walk carefully afterward, owing to the droppings on the path left behind by my cackling disorganized cheerleaders.

I always thought we had the biggest Cornish hens and leghorns. They seemed awfully heavy when I had to catch them at four in the morning to put them in gunny bags so that they could be transported to the chicken factory to be dressed. This is where they were placed in a centrifuge and whirled around so fast that the feathers flew away from their chicken bodies. I think death came before dizziness. I guess that they didn't mind being called dressed when in reality they were actually stark naked. We dressed a few at home as well, but possibly they didn't look as formal!

Here I learned about the profession of chicken catcher. This is a person who catches the chicken between the fingers in a dark room (chickens can't see in the night) and puts them in boxes before they are transported in the back of the trucks. Most of these people get paid by the number of boxes they fill with chickens rather than by the hour. My patient was very fast. He was hit on the head with a two-by-four by one of the men of lesser dexterity.

My son and I fished in most of the lakes from Oshkosh to Eau Claire during our stay in Wisconsin. People often asked me whether I was fishing for muskie or walleye. I never knew which fish was going to take my bait. All night crawlers looked identical to me, but I guess the fish knew the difference between corn flakes and honey roasted. It is only recently that the genetic identity of the night crawlers is being recognized. I never was very discriminating regarding the names of the fish. I was easily satisfied even just by a tug on the line. At the end of the day, if we didn't get anything, we stopped by a place just outside Wausau. We caught many sunfish. That made us feel like we had a successful day. This was our secret place. We never shared the direction to the spot with anyone else. We cleaned the fish together. My son had fun doing surgery on the fish.

I learned to ride a snowmobile. We learned about milking cows, growing corn, and combines. My neighbor ran his combine with the headlight on, and I treated him for his back condition. He taught me about ginseng and its medicinal and potential economic values. He thought there was more money in sex-oriented plants than in corn, which, unfortunately, had not been used for sex yet that we knew.

We talked about the hard work a farmer has to do to make a living and the fact that he never gets a vacation, because he has to milk his cows twice daily. He told me about the operation of a cheese factory. He liked the idea that Senator Proxmire had pushed the nutritional value of cheese to the young soldiers, but he was afraid that this policy might have to be adjusted when America gets fatter. He gave me a little whey for my

Arnold everyday, and he always drove the milk truck on my driveway to press the snow down so I could drive my car out of the garage.

On Friday nights, my girl and I often went to a tavern for a drink. I didn't realize that I was not welcome until one day someone had clipped all four of my tires. This, I learned later, was because the owner's brother who is a painter was disgruntled for not being hired to paint my house. I thought that he gave us an exorbitant bid owing to the fact that I was a doctor. I painted my house myself with a spray gun in one afternoon. However, it took us three months to scrape the windows clean. I had neglected to cover them during my experimental money-saving scheme. I was short on time as well.

I remember the smell of pine when I walked in my yard in the morning. This was in Chapel Hill in 1973. Just 15,000 students, faculty, and Dean Smith, the basketball coach, a true southern gentleman. I got to know him through the students whom he loved, and the feeling was mutual. Here, as I taught and practiced my specialty, I learned to say "peecan pa" and learned to eat persimmon pudding. I listened to Ricky Skaggs, "If you are going to cheat—don't cheat in your home town," and the yodel of Slim Whitman. A woman once asked me to be sure that she didn't get transfused with a black person's blood during an operation. I reassured her that I would be sure that no harm would come to her in the event that such a mishap occurred. I recall one night, soon after I had arrived, getting a phone call from the emergency room about a child who had fallen off a "haacher." I was not familiar with the word, so I asked him to say it slowly, to which he repeated "haacher" slowly but louder. I reminded him that it was not a hearing problem, and if he would spell it for me, perhaps I would understand better. It was clear that the word in contention was "high chair." I acknowledged that I needed some adjustment, as well as reorganization in the auditory and word recognition part of my brain. I enjoyed working with Dr. J. Gregg and Dr. G. Dugger. I learned new concepts of pain. We shared with each other some techniques of performing fusion of the neck.

In North Carolina, we saw copperheads. We also saw water moccasins on our property as we cleared some of it during the summer. I played tennis outside on the day before Christmas. Now, that was quite different from the time in Columbus. On occasion, we built a fire between the bricks and heated fresh oysters. We pitched the shells over our shoulders in our field as we ate the fresh baked oysters. We camped. We walked on the beautiful white beaches and sometimes went skinny-dipping when there was no one around. We flew kites on the dunes of Kitty Hawk. I often looked at my girl's enticing hips. She was busy swinging them while tugging and twisting the rolling pin full of strings from side to side. We held hands. We made heel marks on the wet sand. Sometimes we chased the birds. I made fake bird-foot marks on the sand. I splashed water just for fun. I often looked back. The next wave always polished the heel marks and wiped the foot marks clean. She would collect shells. Sometimes she even brought them home. We made sand castles, but I always invaded hers. She let me! What I liked most was that I didn't have to do anything to please her. She was just happy. We bought fish and cooked it on a grill outside under the canopy of moonlight that glittered with a thousand stars. We sat touching each other as we laughed, remembering some silly stuff. We made love in the bed made by the sound of the cheerful and persistent waves of the ocean. I watched the waves that always tried to catch up, but invariably receded in their attempts to reach the shore. I loved the sprinkling of the spray of laughter the ocean threw toward us as it rolled over each time.

• • • • •

I live on a small property in Kentucky. I have lived here more than twenty-three years. This is my home, where I have friends who truly care and take care of me. We had Goldie the chicken who was a pet of my girl until a red fox got her. This chicken sat on her shoulder. It walked with her and even lay down to sunbathe on the chair by her side. Then we had Lassie, a collie, of course, who followed her. They played ball together, and Lassie gave her company when I was gone. I work quite a bit outside the country, but when I am home I eat lunch with my friends. I go to the post office, the laundry, and the bank. Sometimes, I go to the grocery and the gas station, but not all on the same day. I feel that I need to save something to fill another day. Whenever I am gone these days, even for a short period, I miss my girl and my old Kentucky home. I read poetry and all the classics again. I enjoy my garden.

After many years of planning and owing to following a strict discipline in my life, now I do not go to work for making a living but I work only for living. I sip a glass of chardonnay and think of T. S. Eliot in "Gerontion":

> She gives when our attention is distracted
> And what she gives, gives with such supple confusions
> That the giving famishes the craving.

While the sun sits on the reclining chair, the shadows get longer. We watch the cardinal perch on the tall sycamore.

129

It attacks its very own shadow on the window on the way to the bird feeder. The squirrel takes a break from its walk on the fence to take a drink from the horses' utensils. The fence is laced with red rhododendrons. The mule rolls in the dirt to get rid of an itch. The rabbit comes out from under the rhododendron bush, takes a quick look to be sure of its safety, then munches on the crocuses and cleans its moustache. The dogwoods and redbuds lengthen their shadowy silhouette in the Kentucky sky as the afternoon slowly slips into the evening gown. I lounge in the lingering sunlight, enjoying the events on the farm as they proceed naturally. There are no whistles to start, and no one wins or loses here. The affable sun imparts a loving effect on the farm as the barrister collie barks to announce the llama's efforts to mate with the sheep. The sheep is sitting down in protest. The woodpecker, the judge wearing a crimson wig, pecks with its gable at the magnolia tree. The verdict by the animal court denounces this nonconsensual public display of intimacy. The donkey, on the other hand, brays in surprise—"It don't think like us and talks funny, too!"

I enjoy the love of my colleagues and my friends, and, most importantly, I enjoy the great American culture, fashions, poetry, and art. America has accepted me and has given me all the opportunities I could have ever imagined. I am happy to have found friends in this country of great innovators where freedom to think exists. More important, freedom to speak and individual rights are honored.

· · · · ·

In the late seventies, I operated on a young man's neck to remove a very difficult spinal cord tumor. He was in his late twenties and already paralyzed. His breathing was affected prior to the operation; therefore, I knew that he would not be able to breathe on his own after the operation. After a long operation through the microscope, he remained on a respirator for several months.

I subsequently placed a phrenic nerve pacer (a stimulator for the nerve that moves the diaphragm, the structure between the chest and the stomach). This would allow him to be independent of the respirator for part of the day. He would also be able to communicate when the tracheotomy was covered. Speech was his only mode of communication because he was paralyzed from below the neck. His mother stayed awake many nights wondering how she would know in case he stopped breathing while she was asleep. This was the first time such a device was used in Kentucky, and, therefore, not knowing anyone here with experience, I contacted the president of AT&T. He was more than thrilled to participate in a real-life drama. He made the necessary contacts with different engineers. The engineers then designed an alarm for adults requiring assisted breathing. This device was very similar to the one for the children in incubators that has been available for a long time. His mother then had some peaceful rest. He requested to see the Pope when the Pope visited in the eighties, but we were not able to organize it. I went to St. Peter's square on a first of January, and I acted as his eyes. I stood next to the photographer because I knew I would have a straight shot. I prayed for him. He loved me much. He was pleased at my efforts. He died about thirteen years later from the numerous complications of being paralyzed. Sometimes we talked about the benefits of our freedom. We were humbled by the exemplary attitude and love the engineers expressed in his case by being there for the sake of brotherhood.

As I close my journal, it seems to me there is an appearance of being rewarded for hard work, but it is clear to me that I have never deserved any rewards, and there are many who work even longer hours than I do. However, many of my goals have been met and aspirations fulfilled. It is even a more interesting fact that most of the aspirations were not even conceptualized. They just happened as I went along the path. I just had fun claiming the events later as though this was something I desired. I claimed responsibility for it to have happened. Even now, I enjoy such deception! I never had a muzzle on my face. I enjoyed eating the grass on both sides of the road. I always tested the strength of the leash as I was being steered. I have enjoyed the freedom to chew at my own pace. I am glad that I learned early on in my life that "it isn't something if it ain't loving." I learned to pray for my patients before any operation I performed. At times, when the patients wished, I prayed with them in the room. I was happy to have been included in the family. I have learned to love my patients. I respect them for trusting me. I have always felt that there cannot be more intimacy than to be able to be inside the body or brain of another person.

I am grateful for having had the opportunity to be so intimate with so many people. Many people have truly loved me. Those who did not, left me. Now, I have understood my loneliness, but most of my life is spent. I wish so many times now that it would be so wonderful if I could have been sweet and kind like those who do not have such a big-named illness like mine. I was pleased that I was not an outcast in a society where so many people are deprived of the joys of living because of an unfortunate handicap.

My defect was not visible by itself, but it was certainly audible. I am starting my twilight years with renewed vigor to work with the Federation of International Education of Neuro-